Seminar Leader's Manual

LEARNING PSYCHOTHERAPY

A Time-efficient, Research-based, and Outcome-measured Psychotherapy Training Program

BERNARD D. BEITMAN, M.D.
and
DONGMEI YUE, M.D.

W. W. Norton & Company
New York   London

Copyright © 1999 by Bernard D. Beitman, M.D., and Dongmei Yue, M.D.

All rights reserved
Printed in the United States of America
First Edition

For information about permission to reproduce selections
from this book, write to
Permissions, W. W. Norton & Company, Inc., 500 Fifth Avenue
New York, NY 10110

Composition by PRD Group
Manufacturing by Hamilton Printing

ISBN 0-393-70305-3 (pbk.)

W. W. Norton & Company, Inc., 500 Fifth Avenue, New York, N. Y. 10110
http://www.wwnorton.com

W. W. Norton & Company Ltd., 10 Coptic Street, London WC1A 1PU

2 3 4 5 6 7 8 9 0

Contents

Introduction 1
    The principles behind the training program 1
    Guidelines for conducting the seminars 2
    Supervision 3
    Trainee selection 4
    Personal therapy 4
    Flow Chart of the Training Sessions 5
    Global Impressions of Trainee's Change 9

Pretraining 11

Module 1   *Verbal Response Modes and Intentions* 13
        Sessions 13

Module 2   *Verbal Response Modes and Intentions* 37
        Sessions 37

Module 3   *Inductive Reasoning to Determine Patterns* 43
        Sessions 43

Module 4   *Strategies for Change* 53
        Sessions 53

Module 5   *Resistance* 67
        Sessions 67

Module 6   *Transference and Countertransference* 71
        Sessions 71

Posttraining 83

Afterword 85

References 87

Answers to Forms

Form 9   *Transcripts of Dr. Beitman's Session (Rating Verbal Response Modes)*   18
Form 10   *Hill's Sample Transcript*   25
Form 12   *Transcripts of Dr. Beitman's Session (Rating Intentions)*   29
Form 15–1   *Inductive Reasoning to Determine Patterns*   48
Form 16–1   *Transcripts for Inductive Reasoning*   49
Form 15–2   *Inductive Reasoning to Determine Patterns*   51
Form 16–2   *Transcripts for Inductive Reasoning*   52
Form 18–1   *Transcripts for Change Strategies*   57
Form 19–1   *Case Vignettes for Change Strategies*   58
Form 18–2   *Transcripts for Change Strategies*   62
Form 19-2   *Case Vignettes for Change Strategies*   63
Form 20   *Resistance Case Vignettes*   69
Form 21   *Resistance Case Vignettes*   70
Form 23   *Relationship Episodes–Class Practice*   78
Form 24   *Relationship Episodes–Homework*   79
Form 28   *Case Vignettes of Transference and Countertransference*   81

Seminar Leader's Manual

LEARNING PSYCHOTHERAPY

Introduction

THE PRINCIPLES BEHIND THE TRAINING PROGRAM

We are attempting to give our trainees a conceptual foundation, a model of psychotherapy, that will serve them well in their clinical work. This foundation is broad and is based on common ideas, strategies, and techniques. In this program, trainees are encouraged to think psychotherapeutically not only in formal psychotherapy but also while consulting with other professionals, doing case management, practicing pharmacotherapy, interacting with supervisors, and working in the emergency department.

Our approach is broad, not deep. It goes across schools rather than down into one or several. We think of this approach as a conceptual basement that is strong and broad but not particularly deep. Trainees gain conceptual skills and learn to think about the basic skills of psychotherapy, but they do not practice specific skills in depth. For instance, we do not extensively practice empathic reflections but demonstrate them and have trainees try a few.

This seminar is analogous to the psychotherapeutic relationship, in that the seminar leader, rather than lecturing, facilitates personal growth in psychotherapeutic knowledge and self-understanding. Instead of passively reading and listening to lectures, trainees are asked to participate in the seminar and to complete homework assignments. Since elements of group process definitely become manifest in the seminar, it offers an exercise in group process as well. Here-and-now reactions to each other and to the seminar leader can also be pointed out for discussion. You may find that this format does not fit closely enough with your own concepts of psychotherapy, and you may wish to alter it.

While the training program has a great many technical requirements and is highly organized, you will still find a great deal of flexibility. This structure plus flexibility model is intended to reflect the reality of psychotherapeutic practice, in which basic concepts are varied depending on the circumstances of the patient and the context in which the patient is functioning, as well as the skill limits and strengths of the therapist. We encourage you to make decisions that you believe will enhance the training of the trainees at your site, rather than sticking blindly to the requirements that we have outlined. Perhaps your variations will prove to be more effective than ours. For example, one trainer had only 15 sessions for an introductory course to be followed by other seminars focusing on various schools and strategies. He was also interpersonally oriented and had some psychotherapy research interests. He selected the "intentions" section of module 1 and the rating of the Rogers' tape from module 2, because the normative data from other sites provided comparison rating for his group; he selected only the introductory text and second session from modules 3 and 4 because these provided a foundation for learning about strategies from different schools. He selected two sessions from module 5 and 3 from module 6, including CCRT (Core Conflict Relationship Theme) training, Analysis of Your Reactions to Other People (Form 26) and Transcripts from Borderline Patients (Form 27), because of his interpersonal interests.

You may also choose from several ways of evaluating your program. We evaluate this training program from three different perspectives, including pre- and post-evaluation (trainees' third session and related forms), Counseling Self-Estimate Inventory (COSE), and Global Improvement of Trainee's Change (GITC). You may want to use all these three evaluations, or simply to use COSE, or to choose your own evaluation from updated research information, or not do evaluations at all. Training evaluation is highly recommended in our training program, because it not only tells us what and how trainees have changed, but also allows trainees to step back and look at themselves, to increase their self-awareness of changing and of their strengths and weaknesses.

GUIDELINES FOR CONDUCTING THE SEMINARS

The seminars are at once didactic learning experiences and group process experiences. The didactic experience can be conceptualized as horizontal—the seminar leader attempts to cover the entire content assigned to that day. The group process experience can be conceptualized as vertical—an in-depth meandering into the many possibilities the case or concept presents. As an example of a horizontal experience, consider the 12 cases of resistance done as homework in the last session of module 5. Here you emphasize the best answer to the questions while minimizing the multiple possibilities represented in the other answers. This exercise indirectly teaches the necessity of selecting only one response in the presence of many alternatives. In contrast, some issues draw unique experiences from the group. For example, again from the resistance module, trainees may find themselves fascinated with the problem of silent patients, perhaps because they have encountered them and been unable to respond effectively. Their different experiences with silent patients can provide the group with many variations on an apparently simple theme.

Therapists encourage patients to reflect on their own experiences. Similarly, you are directly and indirectly asking trainees to step back from their own thinking, feeling, and behavior during each of these modules. What verbal response modes do they already use but have not labeled? What are they intending when they respond to a patient? How well is the working alliance developing not only from the patient's perspective but from their own? What patterns of dysfunction do they see in their own lives as well as their patients? What change mechanisms have they and their relatives tried to use? What stops them from learning psychotherapy? What is the range of their "nonprofessional" responses to patients and to colleagues? Repeatedly, we are asking them to activate and develop their observing selves.

SUPERVISION

Supervision of trainees in the standard one-on-one mode has remained the standard method across most training programs. Unfortunately, supervision tends to be unregulated, with training programs leaving the content and methods to the individual supervisor's discretion. Although supervision may be seen to in some ways mimic the psychotherapeutic process and to follow its four stages, the clarification of objectives for supervision remains an important task for any effective training program. In this preliminary description of our training program, let us briefly outline the manner in which the supervisory process parallels the didactic program.

An integrative supervisor should tailor the supervisory experience to the educational and interpersonal needs of each supervisee. The supervisee should be carefully engaged in the supervisory relationship, with attention paid to elements of the working alliance, transference and countertransference responses, and mutual liking or disliking. The supervisor should carefully evaluate the strengths of the supervisee and attempt to identify areas of weakness where goals might be defined and pursued. These areas of strength and weakness can be highlighted through discussion of cases, preferably by the trainee but also possibly by the supervisor. Transference reactions in the form of blocks to learning from the supervisor and countertransference reactions to patients may also offer valuable learning opportunities. However, discussion should not venture into the supervisee's personal life. It would appear useful to apply measures of relationship strength used for patient-therapist interactions to the supervisory relationship.

Each supervisor in this training program should bring into the supervisory sessions elements of the modules that the trainee has already studied and is currently studying. Verbal response modes and intentions, the objectives of the first module, can easily be integrated into discussions focused on audio- or videotapes. The strength of the working alliance can be addressed through direct questions to the patient about agreement between patient and therapist concerning the three subgoals of the working alliance: task, bonds, and goals. The transcripts from the trainee's pre-module patients provide ample opportunities to discuss verbal response modes, intentions, and the working alliance, as well as ideas from the subsequent modules. Supervision should be vertical, providing in-depth experiences using not only trainee transcripts but also case vignettes from each of the modules.

TRAINEE SELECTION

Some authors argue that certain therapist personality characteristics are prerequisites for psychotherapy training (Dobson & Shaw, 1993; Garfield & Bergin, 1971; Garfield & Kurtz, 1976). Training may help an individual enhance and refine a quality like empathy, but it cannot supply what does not exist in the first place (Sakinofsky, 1979). This issue is critical, because research has established that therapists' personal qualities are highly correlated with measures of the helping alliance (Luborsky, McLellan, Woody, O'Brien, & Auerbach, 1985).

Dobson and Shaw (1993) point out that the ability to build sound therapeutic relationships is an aspect of therapist functioning that is relatively immutable during training. They believe that in cognitive therapy sound relationship-building ability should be a selection factor rather than a training issue. Luborsky (1993) notes that more research is needed to determine whether relationship skills can be taught. Binder and Strupp (1993) write that, in their training of therapists in psychodynamic and short-term therapy, they were not able to effectively teach relationship skills, particularly the management of negative therapeutic reactions. Breunlin, Schwartz, and Krause (1989) found that, in the training of family therapists, 50% of the outcome variability was related to preexisting factors (e.g., initial knowledge, family experiences such as being married and/or having children, and previous experience in individual therapy).

Can trainees learn relationship skills? The answer to this crucial quesion depends on how relationship-building skills are defined. Training programs should be able to improve the ability to listen, to reflect back feelings, thoughts, and experiences, and to communicate ideas more effectively. However, training programs cannot teach compassion and empathy. Furthermore, it may well be that marriage and parenthood provide experiences of empathy, compassion, and communication far more effectively than training programs.

PERSONAL THERAPY

Research suggests that psychoanalytic and humanistic practitioners are most likely to have had personal therapy, while eclectic practitioners are less likely to have done so, and cognitive and behavioral therapists even less likely (Robertson, 1995). Robertson (1995) also concluded that those who have had personal therapy are more likely to view personal change as difficult and risky than are practitioners who have not had personal therapy; they are also more likely to believe that therapy strengthens self-awareness, self-nurturance, and self-disclosure. Perhaps, having experienced the role of patient, these therapists understand how valuable the therapeutic relationship is to the patient, because of their awareness of the vulnerability and susceptibility to influence inherent in that role. Whether personal therapy is a decisive contributor to increasing therapeutic effectiveness has yet to be determined by research.

Flow Chart of the Training Sessions

PRETRAINING	Seminar Leader's Tasks	Homework
Session 1	Introduce the 6 modules of the training program, training methods, the goals of the training program, and the requirements for trainees (see the Introduction to the training program). Be sure trainees complete Form 1 and COSE (Counseling Self-Estimate Inventory, Pretraining) within the session. Collect these forms after the session.	X
Session 2	Review directions for the third session audiotape or videotape, emphasizing how to use following pretraining forms: Form 2, Form 3-a, Form 3-b, Form 4-1, Form 4-2, Form 5, Form 6, Form 7, and Patient Consent Forms appropriate to your site. We recommend you set a deadline for them to complete these two sessions (4–6 weeks).	Have two psychotherapy third sessions audiotaped or videotaped and relevant forms completed.
Session 3 (optional)	Gather trainees' feedback about their third session experiences. Keep contact with trainees between session 2 and 3 to monitor progress. Collect the audiotapes or videotapes and the forms distributed in session 2. Prepare 1–2 page extract from one transcript of one of a third session from each trainee and compile them for use in session 5 of module 1. Ask trainees to preview module 1 introduction.	Preview module 1 introduction.
MODULE 1		
Session 1	Go through module 1 introduction and teach verbal response modes (Form 8).	Complete Form 9.
Session 2	Discuss Form 9 with the group.	Complete Form 10.
Session 3	Discuss Form 10 with the group.	Read Form 11.
Session 4	Teach intentions (Form 11).	Complete Form 12.
Session 5	Discuss Form 12 with the group. Distribute the transcript extracts of trainees' third session.	Rate group members' verbal response modes and intentions in transcript excerpts.
Session 6	Discuss the rating of their own verbal response modes and intentions.	X
Session 7	Have trainees complete COSE (post-module 1) and GI post-module 1 during the session and collect them. Continue the discussion of trainees' verbal response modes and intentions.	Preview module 2 introduction.
MODULE 2	Complete Global Impressions of Trainees's Change (GITC) after module 1.	

Session 1	Review the introduction to discuss working alliance. Trainees view the videotape of Rogers' session with Gloria if it has been purchased by your institution. If not, select another tape.	Watch Rogers' session and then use Form 13 to rate his working alliance.
Session 2	Discuss trainees' rating on Rogers' working alliance. Distribute the videotape of Beitman's session with MF to trainees. Collect Form 13 for rating Rogers' session and the tapes after the session.	Watch Beitman's session and use Form 13 to rate Beitman's working alliance with MF.
Session 3	Guide the discussion of Beitman's working alliance. Collect Form 13 for rating Beitman's session and tapes after the session. Do statistics of trainees' ratings for Rogers' and Beitman's working alliances, and trainees' and their patients' ratings of working alliance of the third sessions in pretraining.	X
Session 4	Distribute the results of statistics of working alliance. Discuss trainees' rating of Rogers and Beitman and compare trainees ratings of their own working alliance with the patients' ratings.	Read Form 14-1 and Form 14-2.
Session 5	Have trainees complete COSE (post-module 2) and GI (post-module 2) during the session and collect them. Discuss Form 14-1 and Form 14-2.	Preview module 3 introduction.
MODULE 3	Complete GITC after module 2.	
Session 1	Go through the introduction to discuss inductive reasoning to define patterns. Review the "cherry pie" introduction to Form 15-1 with the group.	Complete Form 15-1. Read Appendix I.
Session 2	Discuss Form 15-1.	Complete Form 16-1.
Session 3	Discuss Form 16-1. Discuss how to do the homework of Form 17.	Complete Form 17.
Session 4	Discuss Form 17 with the group.	X
Session 5	Bring Beitman's videotapes with MF and MC. Or use tapes of your own faculty. After watching the two tapes, discuss the patients' patterns with the group.	Complete Form 15-2.
Session 6 (optional)	Session 6 is optional depending on whether or not trainees want to see additional psychotherapy sessions from therapists at your site.	X
Session 7	Discuss Form 15-2 with the group.	Complete Form 16-2.
Session 8	Have trainees complete COSE (post-module 3) and GI (post-module 3) during the session and collect them. Discuss Form 16-2 with the group.	Preview module 4 introduction.

MODULE 4	Complete GITC after module 3.	
Session 1	Go through the module 4 introduction.	Read module 4 introduction, Appendix II and III.
Session 2	Continue to discuss the introduction. Demonstrate how to do Form 18-1.	Complete Form 18-1.
Session 3	Discuss Form 18-1.	Complete Form 19-1.
Session 4	Discuss Form 19-1.	X
Session 5	Bring the videotape for module 4. Guide the discussion after watching each videotape vignette.	X
Session 6	Continue to watch videotapes and guide the discussion. /	Complete Form 18-2.
Session 7	Discuss Form 18-2.	Complete Form 19-2.
Session 8	Have trainees complete COSE (post-module 3) and GI (post-module 3) in the session and collect them. Discuss Form 19-2.	Preview module 5 introduction.
MODULE 5	Complete GITC after module 4.	
Session 1	Go through the module 5 introduction with the group.	Complete Form 20
Session 2	Discuss Form 20.	Complete Form 21.
Session 3	Have trainees complete COSE (post-module 5) and GI (post-module 5) in the session and collect them. Discuss Form 21.	Preview module 6 introduction.
MODULE 6	Complete GITC after module 5.	
Session 1	Go through module 6 introduction with the group.	Read module 6 introduction.
Session 2	Continue to go through module 6 introduction with the group.	Read module 6 introduction.
Session 3	Teach CCRT method. Go through Form 22. Teach how to use CCRT to rate transference (Form 23).	Complete Form 24.
Session 4	Discuss Form 24.	Read Appendix IV and complete Form 25.
Session 5	Discuss Appendix IV and Form 25.	X
Session 6	Bring Beitman's videotapes with J and the videotape of Beitman's self-description of his reaction to the patient. Watch videotapes and discuss transference and countertransference.	Complete Form 26.

Session 7	Discuss Form 26.	Complete Form 28.
Session 8	Discuss Form 27.	Complete Form 29.
Session 9	Discuss Form 28.	
Session 10	Complete Form 29.	
Session 11	Have trainees complete COSE (post module 6) and GI (post module 6) during the session and collect them. Discuss post-module and review the training program.	X
POSTTRAINING	Complete GITC after module 6.	
Session 1	Give the directions about how to have their third session audiotaped or videotaped and how to use the following Posttraining Forms: Form 2, Form 3-a, Form 3-b, Form 4-1, Form 4-2, Form 5, Form 6, Form 7, Patient Consent Forms (for your site). Distribute two blank audiotapes or videotapes. We recommend you set a deadline for them to complete these two sessions; usually it takes about two months at our site).	Have the third psychotherapy session audiotaped or videotaped with two patients and complete the forms.
Session 2	Keep contact with trainees between session 1 and 2. Collect the audiotapes or videotapes and the forms distributed in session 1. Make sure trainees return all forms. Discuss the differences between their pretraining and post-training psychotherapy sessions and the impact on them of this training program.	

Global Impressions of Trainee's Change

Trainee's Name _____   Rater _____

Baseline Evaluation: (After module 1)   Date _____

Given your experience with this psychotherapy trainee, how good a therapist is he/she?

- ① ☐ Excellent
- ② ☐ Very good
- ③ ☐ Good
- ④ ☐ Not good/not poor
- ⑤ ☐ Poor
- ⑥ ☐ Very poor

Global Improvement After Each Module:

After module 2 (Date_____)

1. Given your experience with this psychotherapy trainee, how good a therapist is he/she?

    - ① ☐ Excellent
    - ② ☐ Very good
    - ③ ☐ Good
    - ④ ☐ Not good/not poor
    - ⑤ ☐ Poor
    - ⑥ ☐ Very poor

2. Compared with his/her ability at the end of module 1 (baseline assessment), how much has he/she changed? Rate total improvement, whether or not it is due entirely to the psychotherapy training program.

    - ① ☐ Much improved
    - ② ☐ Moderately improved
    - ③ ☐ Minimally improved
    - ④ ☐ No change
    - ⑤ ☐ Minimally worse
    - ⑥ ☐ Moderately worse
    - ⑦ ☐ Much worse

After module 3 (Date_____)

1. Given your experience with this psychotherapy trainee, how good a therapist is he/she?

    - ① ☐ Excellent
    - ② ☐ Very good
    - ③ ☐ Good
    - ④ ☐ Not good/not poor
    - ⑤ ☐ Poor
    - ⑥ ☐ Very poor

2. Compared with his/her ability at the end of module 1 (baseline assessment), how much has he/she changed? Rate total improvement, whether or not it is due entirely to the psychotherapy training program.

    - ① ☐ Much improved
    - ② ☐ Moderately improved
    - ③ ☐ Minimally improved
    - ④ ☐ No change
    - ⑤ ☐ Minimally worse
    - ⑥ ☐ Moderately worse
    - ⑦ ☐ Much worse

After module 4 (Date_____)

1. Given your experience with psychotherapy trainee, how good a therapist is he/she?

   ① ☐ Excellent
   ② ☐ Very good
   ③ ☐ Good
   ④ ☐ Not good/not poor
   ⑤ ☐ Poor
   ⑥ ☐ Very poor

2. Compared with his/her ability at the end of module 1 (baseline assessment), how much has he/she changed? Rate total improvement whether or not it is due entirely to the psychotherapy training program.

   ① ☐ Much improved
   ② ☐ Moderately improved
   ③ ☐ Minimally improved
   ④ ☐ No change
   ⑤ ☐ Minimally worse
   ⑥ ☐ Moderately worse
   ⑦ ☐ Much worse

After module 5 (Date_____)

1. Given your experience with this psychotherapy trainee, how good a therapist is he/she?

   ① ☐ Excellent
   ② ☐ Very good
   ③ ☐ Good
   ④ ☐ Not good/not poor
   ⑤ ☐ Poor
   ⑥ ☐ Very poor

2. Compared with his/her ability at the end of module 1 (baseline assessment), how much has he/she changed? Rate total improvement whether or not it is due entirely to the psychotherapy training program.

   ① ☐ Much improved
   ② ☐ Moderately improved
   ③ ☐ Minimally improved
   ④ ☐ No change
   ⑤ ☐ Minimally worse
   ⑥ ☐ Moderately worse
   ⑦ ☐ Much worse

After module 6 (Date_____)

1. Given your experience with this psychotherapy trainee, how good a therapist is he/she?

   ① ☐ Excellent
   ② ☐ Very good
   ③ ☐ Good
   ④ ☐ Not good/not poor
   ⑤ ☐ Poor
   ⑥ ☐ Very poor

2. Compared with his/her ability at the end of module one (baseline assessment), how much has he/she changed? Rate total improvement whether or not it is due entirely to the psychotherapy training program.

   ① ☐ Much improved
   ② ☐ Moderately improved
   ③ ☐ Minimally improved
   ④ ☐ No change
   ⑤ ☐ Minimally worse
   ⑥ ☐ Moderately worse
   ⑦ ☐ Much worse

Pretraining

Pretraining has two purposes: (1) to introduce the modules to the trainees and (2) to help each trainee to obtain an audiotape of the third session from two psychotherapy relationships, which will serve as a baseline for later comparison to two posttraining relationships tapes. The training program is intended to provide feedback to trainees and to provide measures of learning.

Session 1

Purpose: To review the general introduction to *Learning Psychotherapy,* focusing on goals (including activation of the observing self and use of the stages of psychotherapy) and requirements of the training program, particularly the details associated with the pre-module.

Some trainees may consider the data collection at baseline and throughout the modules to be research. This activity is more accurately seen as program evaluation, similar to the growing requirement that all clinical practices be similarly evaluated.

Students are asked to complete Therapist Training Background (Form 1) and Counseling Self-Estimate Inventory (COSE-Pretraining) during the session (leave at least 20 minutes to complete the forms). These forms serve as part of the baseline information. We recommend that a file be kept for each trainee.

Session 2

Purpose: To introduce the forms that need to be completed after trainees' third psychotherapy session.

The amount of paperwork appears significant, but careful reading of this section will demonstrate the value of completing it. In session 2 of pretraining (*Learning Psychotherapy,* page 11), we list the details of how and when to use these forms; trainees should read the pretraining description to check which forms are to be completed at what times. Most trainee questions center around how to use Form 6 (Rating the Therapist's Intentions) and Form 7 (Patient Reaction Systems). The group should carefully read the directions on the top of the first page of each form. In order to help trainees understand these two forms, you also can quickly go through the definitions of therapist intentions and the patient reaction system. Keep in mind that these forms will be studied in great depth in module 1. To ensure that patients understand the categories of the Patient Reaction System, trainees might be advised to go through it with them before they review the third session together. The pairing of these two exercises after each therapist turn forces therapists to step back from their responses not only to wonder what they were intending but also to discover how the patient responded. Upon these building blocks, therapeutic relationships and fulcrums for change are established.

Trainees may have difficulty finding psychotherapy patients. Keep in mind that patients can come from many different sources, including inpatient units, consultation services, undergraduate and graduate student counseling services, case management, etc. The sessions need not be 40–50 minutes long (20–30 may be sufficient), nor need they be separated by one week (a day may be sufficient). Some trainees will continue past the third session while others will stop there.

Questions often asked by our trainees include:

1. One of my friends is under a great deal of stress. May I use him as one of my patients? *Answer:* No. Establish the working alliance with a person who becomes your patient.
2. Why choose the third session? *Answer:* Most psychotherapy researchers use the third or fourth session for early analysis because the relationship is fairly well established and they are no longer limited to history-taking and assessment.
3. How do we do the audiotaping? *Answer:* You may need to audiotape all three sessions just to get used to taping. Patients may have a variety of odd reactions to the audiotaping and you may be overly self-conscious for a while. The consent form may be filled out once for all three sessions.
4. Why should we audiotape now when we know so little about psychotherapy? *Answer:* Much of your behavior as a therapist depends on the experiences and knowledge you already have. We want you to be able to see the difference between your abilities now and your abilities when the modules are completed. At that time you will do another set of third session audiotapes with two additional patients. In a perfect world, these patients would closely resemble the patients you will be seeing in the pretraining, but this variable is very difficult to control.

After the second session in pretraining, you should keep in touch with trainees. Make sure they have their third sessions audiotaped and check that they have returned the completed forms and audiotapes before they enter module 1. We suggest you set a deadline for trainees to complete the work on these two third sessions.

Note: One of each trainees' third sessions should be transcribed. The administrative assistant can extract parts of the dialogue from each trainee's transcription and put them together for use in learning verbal response modes and intentions in module 1.

Session 3 (Optional)

This session can be used to gather trainees' feedback about their third sessions and to ask trainees to preview the module 1 text.

MODULE 1

Verbal Response Modes and Intentions

SESSIONS

Session 1

Purpose: To go through the module 1 text in *Learning Psychotherapy* and review the verbal response modes. Verbal response modes reflect communication patterns of the therapist that are pantheoretical and fundamental to all schools of psychotherapy. We teach verbal response modes to broaden trainees' communication styles by learning new response categories and becoming increasingly aware of verbal response modes they already use but have not labeled.

(For this session and for most of the other sessions of each module, the paragraphs below are numbered as follows: Paragraph #1 contains instructions to you about how to conduct the session. Paragraph #2 contains experiences from our trainees. Paragraph #3 describes the homework for the next session.)

1. You discuss the definitions of each of the verbal response modes (Form 8) with the group. You can ask one trainee to read the definition and comment and then ask others to comment. Trainees will disagree on several verbal response modes. These disagreements are critical for the learning process, since resolution requires careful consideration of the elements of each mode. You should help them to clarify, distinguish, and compare any verbal response modes that they have trouble understanding.

2. Some have trouble discriminating between *reflections* and *restatements*, *interpretations* and *confrontations*. They are likely to apply their own definitions if they do not read the definitions carefully. You may help them to clarify by emphasizing the following: Reflection is defined primarily by its attention to *emotion*; restatement is characterized by its repeating what the patient said; interpretation differs in going beyond what the client consciously recognizes to make some connection between isolated statements and events; confrontation is distinguished by its containing two parts, the first of which is usually a statement, and the second part of which usually begins with the word "but."

Our trainees report that the verbal response mode categories help them categorize responses they have already being making. Some realize that all they have been doing is gathering information through questions.

3. Homework: Trainees are asked to complete Form 9, the object of which is to categorize the verbal response modes from a session of Dr. Beitman's.

Session 2

Purpose: To review trainees' ratings of Form 9. The discussion is intended to broaden the range of their response modes by forcing them to discriminate among and between complex response modes, especially restatement, reflection, interpretation, and confrontation.

1. Trainees are asked to read aloud each of the therapist's verbal response units and then to report and justify their ratings. Disagreements often reflect trainees' difficulty understanding the response modes; discussion further clarifies the definitions. The ratings supplied by the authors (Answers to Form 9) serve as reference points that can help you to facilitate the discussion. Keep in mind that some of the "answers" may not be absolutely correct. It is the struggle to comprehend through dialogue that provides the greatest learning. During the discussion, you should ask trainees to go back to the actual definitions in Form 8, especially when the comments begin to wander.

2. Again, disagreements often occur between restatement and reflection, interpretation and confrontation, and open question and closed question. For example, our trainees have struggled with the phrase, "So this week you got in touch with your anger." Is this a restatement or reflection? While examining the phrases "it was my impression last time that you were skating on top of it but never or rarely visiting it" from the sixth therapist speaking turn, trainees have struggled with differentiating interpretation from reflection. These and subsequent discussions lead to a focus on feelings and a beginning understanding of the concept of interpretation as causal and somewhat beyond the patient's current awareness. The struggle to understand through discussion seems to further understanding in a way that could not be achieved by didactic presentation alone.

3. Homework: Trainees complete Hill's Sample Transcript Form 10 for rating verbal response modes.

Session 3

Purpose: to discuss trainees' rating of Form 10. The exercise of Form 10 is same as Form 9.

1. The procedure of this session is similar to the previous one.

2. Trainees generally report greater ease in selecting the Hill verbal response mode categories compared to the Beitman transcript of the previous session. Discussion centers around some lingering disagreements in distinguishing modes. For example, is CO (counselor statement) "I hear you saying that you would feel freer to live your own life if you weren't living at home" a restatement, reflection, or interpretation?

3. Homework: Trainees review Form 11 (definitions of therapist intentions).

Session 4

Purpose: To review Form 11. Intentions describe the therapist's objectives for each intervention. The study of one's intentions activates the observing self. Teaching intentions can increase trainees' ability to ask, "What do I want to accomplish?" within the session in any given moment.

1. The group discusses each intention one by one. Encourage the trainees' comments on each intention and help them to distinguish among intentions that can be easily confused, including *change, challenge,* and *reinforce change; support* and *catharsis; focus* and *clarify,* and so on. Help the trainees distinguish between the verbal response modes and the intentions and understand the relationship between them. Various response modes could be used to accomplish the same intentions; for instance, the therapist could help the patient explore feelings and behaviors through an *open question, interpretation, restatement,* or *confrontation.* On the other hand, each response mode can be used to implement several different intentions; for example, open questions can be used with the following intentions: *get information, cognition, feelings, catharsis,* and *relationship.*

2. This list of 20 definitions provides an outline of the techniques of psychotherapy. In our experience, for example, "set limits" often leads to a discussion of the therapeutic contract and the handling of telephone calls with borderline patients. "Focus" helps to differentiate the naive, untrained listener from a more directing interviewer. "Cognitions" leads to a discussion of cognitive therapy and more generally to the overarching influence of one's worldview on interaction. "Self-control" initiates discussion of responsibility and the recognition that therapists can only influence the person in the office; the person must be responsible for change outside the office. We have added "interpersonal" to the list, since we believe that it deserves its own category, rather than being placed as an add-on to the "behavior" intention category where it was originally.

3. Homework: Trainees complete Form 12, which is the same transcript contained in Form 11. This time the trainees rate intentions rather than verbal response modes.

Session 5

Purpose: To review Form 12. It is from Dr. Beitman's session with a patient. This videotape is to be shown in module 2. It is ideal if each site develops its own tape and transcript, since intentions are best discussed with the person doing the intending—the seminar leader.

1. Trainees are asked to report and justify their ratings. You report the intentions reported by Dr. Beitman (Answers to Form 12).

2. The trainees often wrestle with defining the primary intention of each therapist speaking turn, as well as with some of the terms. For example, "focus" resembles "clarify." You can ask the group to reread the definition and use diagrams or visual images to suggest that "clarify" means sharpening the current field of discussion, while "focus" means shifting to another field of discussion.

Trainees appear to learn from the struggle to understand and discriminate more clearly among various intentions, including: *feeling* and *cathart, cognition* or *behavior* and *insight, behavior* and *reinforce change, resistance* and *challenge*. "Insight" is particularly problematic, because trainees have had little experience with psychodynamic interpretations. We have described it as making connections between the past and present and then left it for discussion in future modules. Our trainees are asked to consider "cognition, feeling, and behavior" as part of defining patterns, not part of change. While "support" is an element of "reinforce change," "reinforce change" is more specific. Trainees are encouraged to generate many answers and then to justify their answers to their colleagues. In this way they begin learning the building blocks of psychotherapeutic intent.

This exercise has proved to be a kind of Rorschach test, as trainees differ in the primary intentions they perceive. For example, one resident in our program saw "support" where others did not.

We prefer to use two sessions for this assignment because trainees need time to think about the purposes of their interventions. Again, right answers are less important than clarifying, focusing, and understanding the potential range of intentions.

3. Homework: Distribute extracts (about 1–2 pages) from trainees' transcripts from the third session of one of their pretraining relationships. Trainees rate the verbal response modes and intentions from each of these excerpts, skipping their own.

Session 6

Purpose: To review selected dialogues from trainees' transcripts for verbal response modes and intentions. This exercise brings home the work of this module by giving each trainee the opportunity to consider what others think of his/her verbal response modes and intentions. Each trainee then must explain and justify his/her responses.

1. Trainees are asked to select one or two lines from their own dialogues. Other trainees then say what they think the verbal response modes and intentions are. Then the trainee-therapist explains his/her own answer. The trainees discuss the differences between their ratings and the therapist's. This comparison can help trainees gain further understanding of their therapeutic intentions by examining how others see them.

2. There is no need for you to define a "right" answer, since the therapist is present to explain his/her intentions. Trainees tend to answer in their own patterns, some seeing support, others seeing insight, and still others seeing change or reinforcing change.

Our trainees find this to be the most useful part of the module, since they can (1) see how others see them, (2) see how others do therapy, and (3) hear the intention directly from the therapist who is right there in the room with them.

Session 7

Purpose: To complete guided questions (GI* Post-module 1) and COSE** (Post-module 1) (the first 20 minutes), to continue the discussion of trainees' verbal response modes and intentions (the next 40 minutes). After the session, you complete GITC (Global Impressions of Trainee's Change, see page 9).

Once again each resident selects a therapist turn. The other group members share their opinions of verbal response modes and intentions, ending with the therapist's describing and explaining his/her intentions.

For homework, trainees need to preview the module 2 text in *Learning Psychotherapy*.

**Guided Inquiry:* After extensive discussion and role playing, Heppner, Rosenberg, and Hedgespeth (1992) developed a semi-structured, open-ended questionnaire called the Guided Inquiry to assess how clients specifically construct and interpret the change process and counselor's behavior over time. It was hoped that data reflecting clients' phenomenological construction of therapeutic events would provide important information about how clients make meaning of major events within counseling. The results from the initial research (Heppner et al., 1992) revealed that the Guided Inquiry provided a rich source of information about clients' construction of the change process in counseling and seemed to add another dimension to understanding the change process. Later research has found the Guided Inquiry to be useful in understanding students' experiences in multicultural training (Heppner & O'Brien, 1997), as well as later qualitative studies of the counseling process (Heppner & Mintz, 1997).

**Counseling Self-Estimate Inventory (COSE).* The COSE operationalizes counseling self-efficacy defined as one's beliefs or judgments about one's capabilities to effectively counsel a client in the near future (Larson & Daniels, 1998). The COSE measures one's self-estimate of future performance; it does not measure counseling performance. It has been shown to relate moderately to counseling performance (Larson, Suzuki, Gillespie, Potenza, Toulouse, & Bechtel, 1992; White, 1996). Scores can range from 37 to 222, with higher scores indicating greater counseling self-efficacy. Larson et al. (1992) reported that the internal consistency was .93 and the three-week test-retest reliability was .87. Validity estimates for the COSE indicate that (a) the COSE and anxiety significantly predicted counselor performance, (b) trainee's COSE scores increased about one standard deviation over practicum, (c) counselors and psychologists reported higher COSE scores than prepracticum trainees, (d) people with at least one semester of supervision report higher COSE scores than people with no supervision, (e) the COSE was postively related to self-esteem, self-evaluation, positive affect, and outcome expectations (Daniels, 1997; Larson et al., 1992; Larson, Cardwell, & Majors, 1996), (f) the COSE was negatively related to anxiety and negative affect (Alvarez, 1995; Daniels, 1997; De Graaf, 1996; Larson et al., 1996; Larson et al., 1992), and (g) the COSE minimally correlated with defensiveness, aptitude, achievement, age, personality type, and time spent as a client and did not appear to differ across sex or theoretical orientation (Alvarez, 1995; Larson et al., 1992).

Larson and Daniels (1998) provided an integrative review of the literature that examined counseling self-efficacy. Larson (1998a, 1998b) described how counseling self-efficacy was embedded in social cognitive theory as presented by Bandura (e.g., 1986) and how self-efficacy is one construct in a larger theory to explain how counselors and therapists learn how to come effective with clients.

ANSWERS TO FORM 9

(Rating Verbal Response Modes)

Each response unit is demarcated with a slash mark. The numbers to the left of the transcript are classifications by trained judges as to the appropriate category for each response unit. Numbers to the left refer to the following categories: 1 = minimal encourager, 2 = silence, 3 = approval-reassurance, 4 = information, 5 = direct guidance, 6 = closed question, 7 = open question, 8 = restatement, 9 = reflection, 10 = interpretation, 11 = confrontation, 12 = nonverbal referent, 13 = self-disclosure, 14 = other.

4, 6	T: I gave you a homework assignment last time. / How many pages do we have here?/
	P: Oh, probably 50.
8, 6, 6	T: Probably 50. / And the homework assignment was to?/ What was the homework assignment?/
	P: Oh, about anger.
7	T: What about anger?/
	P: Describe my feelings about anger.
8, 7	T: Your feelings about anger. /And, what happened?/
	P: As I began writing, I just went ohoooooo, and all these things from my childhood popped out, and I got in touch with my anger. (*laughs*)
8	T: (*Laughs*) You got in touch with your anger./
	P: Yea, I got in touch with my anger.
9, 8, 7	T: It was my impression last time that you were skating on top of it but never or rarely visiting it. / So this week you got in touch with your anger. / What was that like for you?/
	P: Well, at first when I was keeping the anger log, I was surprised, but then as I watched my pattern I noticed anger would arise and immediately I would squash it. (*coughs*) And so, I think it was Thursday when my mother was doing a number on me at the hospital, and I just said that's enough. And so, (*coughs*)
6	T: Do you want some water?/
	P: Yeah, maybe it would be good. I'm sorry. And ah, then I called both my sisters and I said that I was going to take a day or two off from going to the hospital. (*cough, cough*) Mother, she is ill, she is dying, but I never failed to do anything she asked me to do, but she begins demanding (pounds fist on chair), throwing fits like a three year old, you know, and "You, give me that," and I thought she wanted her tissues so I handed her the tissues. "No, no," but she wanted the lid that went on the hotplate. And so,

	when I gave her the tissues she threw it and "no, no, no" she says, and she is still pointing.
1	T: All right./
	P: So I stood up to her. I put the tissues back on the tray and I said, "Well, damn Mother, don't wait a minute, that'd be awful." And she looked at me like "what's going on here?"
8, 9, 8, 7	T: So you told your mother to cool it./ And that's a new experience for you. A relatively new experience for you. / So you at that moment decided not to go after what she was asking you to do. / Now, I'm curious about what that felt like for you too./
	P: Well, at the time I was just angry. I wasn't into evaluating myself. I was just angry.
8	T: Just angry./
	P: At that moment, I decided I was doing part of this homework assignment, that I had a right to anger as much as anyone else. If other people are angry, I make excuses for them. They're tired, sick, or something. And then I realized, well how many of them make excuses for you? How many are willing to say, "Oh, you're angry."
6	T: If you express some kind of irritation?/
	P: Um hmm. (Yes).
8	T: You wrote in your diary that when you were growing up you were not permitted to have anger./
	P: The messages to me in my childhood were that I had no right to my feelings. One time, I was lying on the bed crying, and my mother said, "What's the matter with you?" And I said, "I'm just so lonely." And she said, "Oh, hell you can't be lonely, you're with kids at school all day."
8	T: So she rejected your feelings./
	P: Right.
8	T: She said your feelings don't count./
	P: I grew up feeling ugly, dumb, lazy, because I couldn't be tired because children don't get tired. I was just lazy. I always figured my father was my buddy because he would sit down and talk to me. But what my father did was philosophize. If I was angry I should understand this person and well, you know, he had a bad marriage, or he was hurt in an accident . . .
10	T: So, your father gave you a model for how to make excuses for other people's feelings and bad behavior, and then you started being able to apply that way of thinking to yourself./
	P: Um hmm (*yes*)

8, 7	T:	You've had more feelings in yourself this week than you have for quite a while,/ what's that been like for you?/
	P:	Well, after I stayed up all Friday night writing this, I began to see these patterns and realized that a child comes into the world as a clean slate and then people start writing on it. And so many of these beliefs that had been pounded into my head were not my beliefs. I felt like there was a chance for me to be free of them to think my own thoughts. It felt great!
8, 9	T:	You seem to describe feeling liberated from other people's imposed rules and attitudes on you,/ and that was a very wonderful feeling for you./
	P:	Um hmm. (*yes*)

* * *

10, 5, 13	T:	And, now you're entering a phase where you're going to be able to express anger differently from before./ Maybe you will need to be able to say something like, "I'm angry," to somebody. Or, "What you said has made me feel angry." / I keep trying to find ways to label your feelings, but I have difficulty./
	P:	(*coughs*) I'm slippery (*laughs*).
8, 8, 13, 3	T:	You're slippery./ Yeah, there are feelings in there, but it's hard to get to them, and / you're a challenge to try to find what you're feeling at any one moment./ You still will have a tendency, I think, to say something sharp./
7	T:	If you were to express your feelings to that friend of your husband who was talking about "when I was working . . . ," and implying that his wife did nothing equivalent taking care of the children and the household, what feeling would you have . . . how would you have labeled your feeling at that moment?/
	P:	I knew why his talk bothered me. He sounded so much like my husband Jim. I knew he hit a raw nerve.
7, 3	T:	How did it make you feel? / And this is going to be a challenge for you./
	P:	Yeah. Right. How did it make me feel?
8, 4, 7	T:	He reminded you of Jim, okay./ This is still intellectual./ How did he make you feel at that moment?/
	P:	The only thing I can think of is anger.
9, 6	T:	You may have thought: "I feel angry at you for what you're saying."/ Now you don't say words like that? "I feel anger."/
	P:	No.

10, 5	T: I mean, you didn't even recognize it before./ But one of the ways that you might safely express the way you feel to someone is to say how you feel./
	P: Oh, what a concept. (*laughs*)
8, 5, 4, 7	T: (*laughs*) Yes, what a concept./ So, I want to see if you could practice that a little bit. To put a label on it because you are slippery around your feelings./ At 48 you've learned a lot of ways to avoid how you feel. There's going to be some work in puncturing through your intellect to get to your emotions./ And, how do you feel about coughing in front of the TV camera?/
	P: I don't like it. It'll be a terrible tape. (*cough*)
7	T: How does it make you feel?/
	P: I don't know. I don't know if I have any feelings about that.
7	T: If someone else was doing something that would look bad, how do you think that person would feel?/
	P: Maybe embarrassed, or ah . . . I basically feel like I'm way on past embarrassment, so (*coughs, coughs, coughs*) so I don't want to ruin the session by coughing all the way through it, so is that embarrassment? I don't know.
8, 4	T: Yeah, embarrassment,/ and maybe a little deeper than that./
	P: When you come from a deeply dysfunctional family as mine, boy you go farther than that to get embarrassed. (*cough*) You know . . .
13, 10, 7	T: No, I don't know. I don't know./ Maybe you don't have to go very far at all to get embarrassed too, which I think is more the case. / If someone was doing something that she couldn't control, that was gonna create embarrassment, how might she feel?/
	P: (*cough*) Embarrassed, I guess. (*cough*)
6,4,6,10,4,7	T: Frustrated? Helpless?/ These are down a little bit lower because you're not embarrassed yet. / Out of control? / These are words that get to feelings that you're not particularly familiar with. / To be able to struggle with feelings means you have to be able to recognize them./ When you were able to be loving to Jim, how did you feel?/
	P: Of course, (*laughs*). I first felt loving when I was going to town and do the shopping and then to the family reunion. I bent down and kissed him and I probably, if anything, felt gratitude that he wasn't going to give me a lot of trouble about it. Because, usually when I leave the house,

	even though he normally doesn't verbally express anything, he acts as if I am doing something wrong or he'll say, "Yeah right." He is aware that I read his body language. I'm much better at other people's feelings than my own.
6	T: What are feelings that other people have?/
	P: (*clears her throat*) Well, I know that Jim feels abandoned when I'm running out of the house and wonders why isn't he enough for me. Why do I have to friends and family to see.
7	T: How does that make him feel, that you have to have other people?/
	P: Well, it makes him feel sad and angry and . . . abandoned.
10, 4, 7	T: Okay, sadness and anger are feelings that people have. You may even have such feelings. / Abandonment can lead to feelings of sadness and anger./ What other feelings do people have?/
	P: Oh, everything from joy, hysteria . . .
8	T: You do hysteria sometimes./
	P: Um hmm (*yes*)
4, 8, 14, 6	T: Joy is a feeling, sadness, anger, hurt are other ones that people have./ So Jim felt hurt that you need to have other people in your life besides him. / All right./ How good are you at picking up your own sadness?/
	P: Oh, pretty good.
6	T: So, you know that one fairly well?/
	P: Um hmm (*yes*)
6	T: How about telling people that you're sad./
	P: Oh, I don't have too much trouble with that. Ah, with the panic attacks, I have had to talk about my feelings, about feeling sad or hurt or ashamed.
8, 9	T: So, those feelings are more accessible to you and easier for you to talk about with people. / So anger is the one that you have the most difficulty with then./
	P: Um hmm (*yes*)
6	T: How good are you at recognizing anger in other people?/
	P: Oh, yeah. Real good.
8, 7	T: You're sensitive to that one too, as I might imagine you would be. / What about being able to say to Jim, "I'm angry with you."/
	P: I can do that.
6	T: Have you done that before?/
	P: Oh, yeah. (*laughs*) No more than 10 million times, but it didn't do any good.

7	T: Now what's the difference between the way you are now about anger and the way you were before?/
	P: You mean when I was repressing it?
10	T: Yes. My impression was that you didn't express anger until it got intense./
	P: Um hmm (*yes*)
8,6,8,10,12,8	T: When you came back from Iowa and boom, blew up at him./ If you change, you may be able to say "I'm angry" over smaller things. / You sound like you may be able to say to him, "I care about you," too. / That other feeling may be coming to the surface as you get more comfortable with your own anger. / You're nodding,/ that's what you experienced recently with him./
	P: Um hmm (*yes*)
6	T: Do you care about Jim?/
	P: Well, as the semantics go I love Jim, I'm not sure I'm in love with Jim, but yes, I've always known I loved Jim, even when I was angry. But the in love romantic feeling is gone.
8, 6	T: But you do love him. / How often do you express that feeling to him?/
	P: Well, it depends on how big a jerk he is? (*laughs*) Since Jim is negative most of the time, I just talk about whatever's going on, which is what we may have for supper that night or what's going on with the kids or mother. So I just stick to daily subjects.
7	T: I'm curious about how this awareness of your anger is going to influence your relationship to him./
	P: I feel the biggest reason I was on such a high as I wrote about anger, was because I was able to take a more clinical view and see everyone's patterns and see that I don't have to be controlled by mother or Jim, my grandmother, and my past. I do know it's going to take work, but at this point I don't give a damn what happens with Jim and I, whether we stay together or whether we break up. Because I finally realized that I am okay on my own, and I would rather be free and living in an efficiency apartment somewhere than to live with Jim and feel miserable. So, basically I don't care.
14, 4, 7, 7	T: Okay. / One final question, and then we will stop for this time. Or two questions really./ What about the spring-summer business and not the winter? / What do you make out of that pattern?/
	P: (*coughs*)

6, 7	T: You had your anxiety in the spring-summer but not during the winter?/ Hard to explain that one still?/
	P: Yeah, after Pat (her chiropractor) did the emotional release thing on me, I started feeling better immediately. I felt better after I was here last time. I felt better as I began to feel like I had a right, if I want to be selfish today. If I want to say, "I'm not going to get out of my nightgown, I'm just gonna lie around, scratch where I want to," you know, then that's okay.
8, 4, 9	T: And that's where you are now. / And now there is an adventure in front of you./ You're not sure where this is going to take you, but you feel liberated and that feels good./
	P: Um hmm (*yes*)
7, 7	T: What about my role in this?/ What do you need from me in the future in regard to helping you? /
	P: I don't know. I guess to keep me from going off the deep end. We still haven't really discussed the safer ways for me to express anger. I can always do the psychologist trick and turn it back around. I'm going to do that on mother the next time she throws one of those fits or demands I do something. I'm going to say, "Mother, I do everything you ask me to, why do you have to be demanding?" Then I'll wait for a reaction. She'll probably throw another fit, but I'll keep asking her that question until maybe she'll say, "Well, that is true. I do get everything I want."
5,4,5,3,8,3,6	T: Well, you may be able to come up with these safer ways of doing them without much help from me./ So, as you know, I'm going to be on vacation for the next couple of weeks. / During that period of time I'd like you to write down examples of the safer expressions of anger. Let's see what you come up with. / You may come up with more than I ever could come up with because you've been so psychologically clever./ Now that you know that you need to develop safe ways of expressing something you are aware of. /I think you will come up with a lot of good ones. So, I'd like to see what you come up with./ All right?

© 1997, Bernard D. Beitman. Department of Psychiatry and Neurology, School of Medicine, University of Missouri-Columbia, One Hospital Drive, Columbia, MO 65212.

ANSWERS TO FORM 10

Each response unit is demarcated with a slash mark. Numbers to the left of the transcript are classifications by trained judges as to the appropriate category for each response unit. Numbers refer to the following categories: 1 = minimal encourager, 2 = silence, 3 = approval-reassurance, 4 = information, 5 = direct guidance, 6 = closed question, 7 = open question, 8 = restatement, 9 = reflection, 10 = interpretation, 11 = confrontation, 12 = nonverbal referent, 13 = self-disclosure, 14 = other.

14, 7	CO: Hello./ Why don't you start out by telling me what is on your mind?/
	CL: I've just been feeling down lately./ I'm having a lot of trouble getting motivated and getting stuff done./ I haven't felt like going to class./ Nothing really interests me./
6	CO: What is your major?/
	CL: I haven't really decided on a major because I haven't found anything that turns me on./
6	CO: Are you living on campus?/
	CL: I'm living at home/ and I feel a lot of pressure on me./ I would like to live in the dorm/ but my parents won't pay for it/ and I don't have the money myself./
1	CO: MmHmm/
	CL: I mean, I live right near campus/ and they say why should you live in a dorm?/ You might as well live at home and save us money./ It is kind of a stifling feeling just being there./
8	CO: You would rather live in a dorm than at home right now./
	CL: I think I would feel more free in a dorm./ I just feel so restricted at home, like they're watching my every move/ and I don't feel free to come and go as I please./ For example, if you want to go out, they always tell me to stay out as late as I want and do what I want, but then the next day they're always asking and checking up on me./ I shouldn't have to put up with that any more at my age./
9	CO: You're angry because they treat you like a little kid./
	CL: Yeah./ I'm not sure how to deal with that./ They're providing me with a place to sleep and helping me out a little with school/ so I feel like I can't say anything to them./

8	CO:	It sounds like you think that you have to stay home and do what they want./
	CL:	Yeah,/ but it's killing my social life./ It's not really what I want to do./ It's even having a bad effect on my schoolwork./
9	CO:	I hear you saying that you would feel freer to live your own life if you weren't living at home./
	CL:	That's true./ But the problem with that is money./ I'm going to school part-time and working part-time and don't have enough money for a dorm or an apartment./ My parents won't give me any more money either./ What really burns me up is that my younger brother is not in school and works and they don't give him any of this crap./
1	CO:	I see./
	CL:	(*pause = 8 seconds*)/ He can do anything he wants, you know, in terms of living at home./ They don't bug him at all about what he's doing and where he's going./ I guess they think that because I'm the oldest and more responsible, I can handle more than he can./ They both had a hard time as kids and they really want me to have what they didn't have./ I guess they think I've got a better chance than my brother does to succeed/ and so they're tougher on me./
12, 9	CO:	Your voice is very loud right now./ You must be very resentful./
	CL:	Well, I just don't want to live their lives for them./ I want to have some fun on my own./
2, 8, 11	CO:	(*silence = 5 seconds*)/ You say you want to move out/ yet you don't./
	CL:	I guess I don't want to disappoint them./ Um, they'd feel real bad if I left/ and
10	CO:	(*pause = 3 seconds*/ I wonder if you're afraid of making the big step of growing up by moving out?/
	CL:	I hadn't thought of it that way./ I don't know if that's exactly it./ I think I'm pretty independent./
4, 8, 11	CO:	Well, let's look at that for a minute./ You say you're independent/ but when your parents tell you to do all these things, you do them./
	CL:	What else can I do?/ What choice do you think I have?/ I'm living there/ and the rule is that I should do what they say as long as I live under their roof./ They might kick me out if I didn't./
13, 13, 13, 10	CO:	You know, when I was your age I had a very difficult time leaving home./ My father had died and my mother

was all alone./ I felt guilty for a long time about leaving her./ I wonder if you're feeling some guilt about growing up and leaving them!/

CL: Well, I do feel guilty about leaving but also angry at them for making me feel this way and for treating my brother differently./ What do you think I ought to do to resolve this?/

5   CO: Maybe it would be a good idea to drop out of school for awhile, get a job, and make enough money to move into your own apartment./

CL: I've thought about that but feel anxious that I'd never go back to school./ But you know, as I think about it, maybe the reason I have so much trouble about motivation in school is because of these conflicts with my parents./

7   CO: What do you mean?/

CL: Well, if I feel like I'm doing everything for them instead of because I want to do it and if there's always this battle over my future, it's pretty hard for me to figure out what I want./

12   CO: When you said that, your forehead wrinkled up and you began to look tearful./

CL: (*silence = 10 seconds*)/

4, 7   CO: We only have a couple of minutes left./ Where would you like to go from here with this problem?/

CL: Do you think it would be worthwhile to talk to someone again?/

7   CO: What do you think?/

CL: You've made me think about some things./ I'm feeling really confused right now./ I wasn't sure before this about seeing you because I didn't know what to expect from this counseling/ but you seem to understand me./ Maybe you can help me figure out some of this mess with my parents and school./

1, 10, 3, 3   CO: Yeah./ It sounds like you have trouble figuring out who you are and what you want out of your life, separate from what your parents want./ That certainly seems like something appropriate to talk about here in counseling./ I think it would be a good idea for you to continue to see me./

CL: I do feel a bit anxious talking to you because it feels like you can see right through me./

13, 13, 3, 3   CO: I feel somewhat anxious right now too./ I usually feel a little tense until I get to know a person and decide

		whether we can work together./ I think you did the right thing by coming in at this point in your life./ You'll probably feel better after talking about your concerns./

CL: I hope so./ I think I'll go home and think about some of these things./ Maybe I'll think about my options about moving out and where I could afford to live./ Maybe I'll talk some to my parents about moving out./ Does that sound like a good idea to you?/

5, 4, 4   CO: Why don't we talk through that at your next session./ We need to stop now./ I'll see you next week at the same time./

CL: Great./ Thank you so much./ Have a nice day./

14, 14, 14   CO: You too./ It's really beautiful weather out./ Feels like spring./

CL: It sure does./ Bye now./

Reprinted with permission from Hill, C. E. (1986). An overview of the Hill Counselor and Client Verbal Response Modes Category Systems. In L. S. Greenberg & W. M. Pinsof (Eds.), *The psychotherapeutic process* (pp.131-159). New York: Guilford.

ANSWERS TO FORM 12

(Rating Intentions)

(To the group leader: we separated each intention by "*" which does not occur in trainee's Form 12. This may facilitate your discussion with the group.) The numbers refer to the following categories: 1 = Set limits, 2 = Get information, 3 = Give information, 4 = Support, 5 = Focus, 6 = Clarify, 7 = Hope, 8 = Cathart, 9 = Cognitions, 10 = Behaviors, 11 = Self-control, 12 = Feelings, 13 = Insight, 14 = Change, 15 = Rein-force change, 16 = Resistance, 17 = Challenge, 18 = Relationship, 19 = Therapist needs, 20 = interpersonal.

2
    T: I gave you a homework assignment last time. How many pages do we have here?*
    P: Oh, probably 50.

6
    T: Probably 50. And the homework assignment was to? What was the homework assignment?*
    P: Oh, about anger.

6
    T: What about anger?*
    P: Describe my feelings about anger.

2
    T: Your feelings about anger. And, what happened?*
    P: As I began writing, I just went ohoooooo, and all these things from my childhood popped out, and I got in touch with my anger. (*laughs*)

12
    T: (*laughs*) You got in touch with your anger.*
    P: Yea, I got in touch with my anger.

15, 12
    T: It was my impression last time that you were skating on top of it but never or rarely visiting it.* So this week you got in touch with your anger. What was that like for you?*
    P: Well, at first when I was keeping the anger log, I was surprised, but then as I watched my pattern I noticed anger would arise and immediately I would squash it. (*coughs*) And so, I think it was Thursday when my mother was doing a number on me at the hospital, and I just said that's enough. And so, (*coughs*)

4
    T: Do you want some water? *
    P: Yeah, maybe it would be good. I'm sorry. And ah, then I called both my sisters and I said that I was going to take a day or two off from going to the hospital. (*cough, cough*) Mother, she is ill, she is dying, but I never failed to do anything she asked me to do, but she begins demanding (*pounds fist on chair*), throwing fits like a three year old, you know, and "You, give me that," and I thought she wanted her tissues so I handed her the tissues. "No, no," but she wanted the lid that went on the hotplate. And so, when I gave her the tissues she threw it and "no, no, no" she says, and she is still pointing.

4	T: All right.*
	P: So I stood up to her. I put the tissues back on the tray and I said, "Well, damn Mother, don't wait a minute, that would be awful." And she looked at me like "what's going on here?".
15, 12	T: So you told your mother to cool it. And that's a new experience for you. A relatively new experience for you. * So you at that moment decided not to go after what she was asking you to do. Now, I'm curious about what that felt like for you too. *
	P: Well, at the time I was just angry. I wasn't into evaluating myself. I was just angry.
6	T: Just angry.*
	P: At that moment, I decided I was doing part of this homework assignment, that I had a right to anger as much as anyone else. If other people are angry, I make excuses for them. They're tired, sick, or something. And then I realized, well how many of them make excuses for you? How many are willing to say, "Oh, you're angry."
6	T: If you express some kind of irritation.*
	P: Um hmm (*yes*).
6	T: You wrote in your diary that when you were growing up you were not permitted to have anger. *
	P: The messages to me in my childhood were that I had no right to my feelings. One time, I was lying on the bed crying, and my mother said, "What's the matter with you?" And I said, "I'm just so lonely." And she said, "Oh, hell you can't be lonely, you're with kids at school all day."
6	T: So she rejected your feelings. *
	P: Right.
6	T: She said your feelings don't count. *
	P: I grew up feeling ugly, dumb, lazy, because I couldn't be tired because children don't get tired. I was just lazy. I always figured my father was my buddy because he would sit down and talk to me. But what my father did was philosophize. If I was angry I should understand this person and well, you know, he had a bad marriage, or he was hurt in an accident. . .
13	T: So, your father gave you a model for how to make excuses for other people's feelings and bad behavior, and then you started being able to apply that way of thinking to yourself. *
	P: Um hmm (*yes*).
6	T: You've had more feelings in yourself this week than you have for quite a while. Well, what's that been like for you? *
	P: Well, after I stayed up all Friday night writing this, I began to see these patterns and realized that a child comes into the

	world as a clean slate and then people start writing on it. And so many of these beliefs that had been pounded into my head were not my beliefs. I felt like there was a chance for me to be free of them to think my own thoughts. It felt great!
6	T: You seem to describe feeling liberated from other people's imposed rules and attitudes on you, and that was a very wonderful feeling for you.*
	P: Um hmm (*yes*).

* * *

15, 14, 6	T: And, now you're entering a phase where you're going to be able to express anger differently from before.* Maybe you will need to be able to say something like, "I'm angry," to somebody. Or, "What you said has made me feel angry." * I keep trying to find ways to label your feelings, but I have difficulty. *
	P: (*coughs*) I'm slippery. (*laughs*)
14, 12, 10	T: You're slippery.* Yeah, there are feelings in there, but it's hard to get to them, and you're a challenge to try to find what you're feeling at any one moment.* You still will have a tendency, I think, to say something sharp.*
12	T: If you were to express your feelings to that friend of your husband who was talking about "when I was working . . . ," and implying that his wife did nothing equivalent taking care of the children and the household, what feeling would you have . . . how would you have labeled your feeling at that moment? *
	P: I knew why his talk bothered me. He sounded so much like my husband Jim. I knew he hit a raw nerve.
12, 14	T: How did it make you feel? * And this is going to be a challenge for you.*
	P: Yeah. Right. How did it make me feel?
12	T: He reminded you of Jim, okay. This is still intellectual. How did he make you feel at that moment? *
	P: The only thing I can think of is anger.
14	T: You may have thought: "I feel angry at you for what you're saying." Now you don't say words like that? "I feel anger." *
	P: No.
15, 14	T: I mean, you didn't even recognize it before. * But one of the ways that you might safely express the way you feel to someone is to say how you feel. *
	P: Oh, what a concept. (*laughs*)
14, 12	T: (*laughs*) Yes, what a concept. So, I want to see if you could practice that a little bit. To put a label on it because you are slippery around your feelings. At 48 you've learned a lot of

	ways to avoid how you feel. There's going to be some work in puncturing through your intellect to get to your emotions.* And, how do you feel about coughing in front of the TV camera? *
	P: I don't like it. It'll be a terrible tape. (*cough*)
12	T: How does it make you feel? *
	P: I don't know. I don't know if I have any feelings about that.
12	T: If someone else was doing something that would look bad, how do you think that person would feel? *
	P: Maybe embarrassed, or ah . . . I basically feel like I'm way on past embarrassment, so (*coughs, coughs, coughs*) so I don't want to ruin the session by coughing all the way through it, so is that embarrassment? I don't know.
12	T: Yeah, embarrassment, and maybe a little deeper than that. *
	P: When you come from a deeply dysfunctional family as mine, boy you go farther than that to get embarrassed. (*cough*) You know . . .
12	T: No, I don't know. I don't know. Maybe you don't have to go very far at all to get embarrassed too, which I think is more the case. If someone was doing something that she couldn't control, that was gonna create embarrassment, how might she feel? *
	P: (*cough*) Embarrassed, I guess. (*cough*)
12, 13, 12	T: Frustrated? Helpless? These are down a little bit lower because you're not embarrassed yet. Out of control? These are words that get to feelings that you're not particularly familiar with.* To be able to struggle with feelings means you have to be able to recognize them.* When you were able to be loving to Jim, how did you feel? *
	P: Of course, (*laughs*). I first felt loving when I was going to town and do the shopping and then to the family reunion. I bent down and kissed him and I probably, if anything, felt gratitude that he wasn't going to give me a lot of trouble about it. Because, usually when I leave the house, even though he normally doesn't verbally express anything, he acts as if I am doing something wrong or he'll say, "Yeah right." He is aware that I read his body language. I'm much better at other people's feelings than my own.
2	T: What are feelings that other people have? *
	P: (*clears her throat*) Well, I know that Jim feels abandoned when I'm running out of the house and wonders why isn't he enough for me. Why do I have to see friends and family.
2	T: How does that make him feel, that you have to have other people? *
	P: Well, it makes him feel sad and angry and . . . abandoned.

12	T: Okay, sadness and anger are feelings that people have. You may even have such feelings. Abandonment can lead to feelings of sadness and anger. What other feelings do people have? *
	P: Oh, everything from joy, hysteria . . .
10	T: You do hysteria sometimes. *
	P: Um hmm (*yes*).
12	T: Joy is a feeling, sadness, anger, hurt are other ones that people have. So Jim felt hurt that you need to have other people in your life besides him. All right. How good are you at picking up your own sadness? *
	P: Oh, pretty good.
12	T: So, you know that one fairly well? *
	P: Um hmm (*yes*).
10	T: How about telling people that you're sad. *
	P: Oh, I don't have too much trouble with that. Ah, with the panic attacks, I have had to talk about my feelings, about feeling sad or hurt or ashamed.
6	T: So, those feelings are more accessible to you and easier for you to talk about with people. So anger is the one that you have the most difficulty with then. *
	P: Um hmm (*yes*).
12	T: How good are you at recognizing anger in other people? *
	P: Oh, yeah. Real good.
4, 10	T: You're sensitive to that one too, as I might imagine you would be.* What about being able to say to Jim, "I'm angry with you." *
	P: I can do that.
2	T: Have you done that before? *
	P: Oh, yeah. (*laughs*). No more than 10 million times, but it didn't do any good.
13	T: Now what's the difference between the way you are now about anger and the way you were before? *
	P: You mean when I was repressing it?
13	T: Yes. My impression was that you didn't express anger until it got intense. *
	P: Um hmm (*yes*).
14, 15	T: When you came back from Iowa and boom, blew up at him. If you change, you may be able to say "I'm angry" over smaller things. * You sound like you may be able to say to him, "I care about you," too. That other feeling may be coming to the surface as you get more comfortable with your own anger. You're nodding, that's what you experienced recently with him.*
	P: Um hmm (*yes*).

2	T:	Do you care about Jim? *
	P:	Well, as the semantics go I love Jim, I'm not sure I'm in love with Jim, but yes, I've always known I loved Jim, even when I was angry. But the in love romantic feeling is gone.
6, 10	T:	But you do love him.* How often do you express that feeling to him? *
	P:	Well, it depends on how big a jerk he is? (*laughs*) Since Jim is negative most of the time, I just talk about whatever's going on, which is what we may have for supper that night or what's going on with the kids or mother. So I just stick to daily subjects.
14	T:	I'm curious about how this awareness of your anger is going to influence your relationship to him. *
	P:	I feel the biggest reason I was on such a high as I wrote about anger, was because I was able to take a more clinical view and see everyone's patterns and see that I don't have to be controlled by mother or Jim, my grandmother, and my past. I do know it's going to take work, but at this point I don't give a damn what happens with Jim and I, whether we stay together or whether we break up. Because I finally realized that I am okay on my own, and I would rather be free and living in an efficiency apartment somewhere than to live with Jim and feel miserable. So, basically I don't care.
2	T:	Okay. One final question, and then we will stop for this time. Or two questions really. What about the spring-summer business and not the winter? What do you make out of that pattern? *
	P:	(coughs)
6	T:	You had your anxiety in the spring-summer but not during the winter? Hard to explain that one still. *
	P:	Yeah, after Pat (her chiropractor) did the emotional release thing on me, I started feeling better immediately. I felt better after I was here last time. I felt better as I began to feel like I had a right, if I want to be selfish today. If I want to say, "I'm not going to get out of my nightgown, I'm just gonna lie around, scratch where I want to," you know, then that's okay.
4, 15	T:	And that's where you are now. And now there is an adventure in front of you.* You're not sure where this is going to take you, but you feel liberated and that feels good. *
	P:	Um hmm (*yes*).
18, 19	T:	What about my role in this?* What do you need from me in the future in regard to helping you? *
	P:	I don't know. I guess to keep me from going off the deep end. We still haven't really discussed the safer ways for me to express

anger. I can always do the psychologist trick and turn it back around. I'm going to do that on mother the next time she throws one of those fits or demands I do something. I'm going to say, "Mother, I do everything you ask me to, why do you have to be demanding?" Then I'll wait for a reaction. She'll probably throw another fit, but I'll keep asking her that question until maybe she'll say, "Well, that is true. I do get everything I want."

15, 3, 15   T: Well, you may be able to come up with these safer ways of doing them without much help from me.* So, as you know, I'm going to be on vacation for the next couple of weeks.* During that period of time I'd like you to write down examples of the safer expressions of anger. Let's see what you come up with. You may come up with more than I ever could come up with because you've been so psychologically clever. Now that you know that you need to develop safe ways of expressing something you are aware of. I think you will come up with a lot of good ones. So, I'd like to see what you come up with. All right?

© 1997, Bernard D. Beitman. Department of Psychiatry and Neurology, School of Medicine, University of Missouri-Columbia, One Hospital Drive, Columbia, MO 65212.

MODULE 2

Working Alliance

SESSIONS

Session 1

Purpose: To go through the text of module 2 in *LP*. The working alliance introduces trainees to the process of engagement in the psychotherapy relationship.

1. Focusing on Bordin's concept of working alliance (for a good explanation of this concept, see Bordin, 1979), group discussion can help the trainees develop a theoretical understanding of the working alliance in psychotherapy. After this discussion, distribute Form 13 (Working Alliance Inventory, WAI) to each trainee.

Play the tape of Dr. Rogers' session* for about 10 minutes and then choose two items from each of the three subscales of the WAI to discuss. Ask trainees to rate each item based on what was shown on the tape and to justify the rating. If the trainees misunderstand the items, provide clarification. They are being trained to be like research associates and to think like researchers about their own efforts. This step can help trainees increase inter-rater reliability. In the real world of research training, these sessions would take much longer and go into much greater depth to obtain inter-rater reliability. Research training promotes "stepping back" from experience in order to objectify observations, in this way promoting activation of the observing self.

You should minimize the inevitable discussion about Rogers' theoretical orientation and therapeutic style because of time constraints. Guide the discussion to focus on their understanding of working alliance, rather than on the patient's problem. The discussion also needs to focus on the differences between the Bordin's working alliance and other relationship components (such as Rogers' emphasis on

---

*You may want to purchase this tape, *Three Approaches to Psychotherapy*, featuring Carl Rogers with "Gloria." It is available for $500 from Psychological and Educational Films, 3334 East Coast Highway, Suite 252, Corona del Mar, CA 92625.

therapist's empathy, Strong's emphasis on patient's belief in therapist's ability, and any other perspectives you have).

2. Trainees often have trouble discriminating between "tasks" and "goals." Clarification of these two terms can lead to better understanding of working alliance.

3. Homework: Arrange for trainees to view the Rogers' tape and ask them to use Form 13 (WAI) to rate the working alliance individually without discussion with colleagues.

Session 2

Purpose: To review trainees' WAI ratings of Rogers' tape as well as to discuss Rogers' style. While rating the therapist's words and behavior, trainees examine in fine detail the concept of working alliance.

1. During the first 40 minutes, the group members discuss their feelings and thoughts about Dr. Rogers' session. The discussion is facilitated by asking trainees to report and then explain their ratings of specific items. Differences among them serve as discussion triggers. Topics to target include: Dr. Rogers' working alliance with emphasis on how he establishes and maintains the therapeutic bond, his style of therapy, and perhaps his reactions to Gloria in the session, including his suggestion that he might like to be a father to her.

During the second 20 minutes, show part of the videotape of Dr. Beitman's third session with MF to the trainees, again using Form 13, WAI. After playing about 10 minutes of the tape of Dr. Beitman's session for the group, choose two items from each of the three subscales of the WAI to discuss. Based on what they just saw, trainees are asked to rate each item and justify their rating. This helps you determine if any trainees are misunderstanding any items, which can then be clarified.

2. Our trainees easily agree that bonds are strong between Rogers and Gloria, but there are sometimes arguments about whether tasks are defined and agreed upon. Some say definitely "yes," because at the end Rogers makes it clear that it is up to Gloria to decide, and some say "no," because the steps she needs to take in order to change have not been defined. There is somewhat more consensus that goals are agreed upon, but when trainees are asked what the goals are, they cannot easily define them.

Trainees often wonder about Rogers' level of activity and speculate that this is probably an early form of psychotherapy. They are not bothered by Rogers' implication that he might like to be her father. Nor are they bothered by the fact that Rogers and Gloria maintained a relationship through letter writing. They are interested in knowing about a lawsuit by Gloria's daughter for misuse of the film, which has been shown in many, many training programs.

Some trainees are impressed with his effective use of silence.

3. Homework: Trainees are asked to watch Beitman's whole session and then rate the working alliance.

Session 3

Purpose: To review responses to WAI of Beitman tape.

1. The seminar leader asks trainees to describe their thoughts and feelings about Beitman's session. The discussion can be facilitated by asking each trainee to select a specific item, and then asking all trainees to explain their ratings and discuss differences. In addition, they can be asked to indicate which subscale the item belongs to. The discussion should include the nature of Beitman's working alliance, with special reference to the three subscales, and the differences between Rogers and Beitman.

2. Our trainees are generally interested in the different level of activity between Rogers and Beitman. They ask about the evolution of psychotherapy and note that patients expect more active interventions now compared to the early 1960s. Agreement on tasks for Beitman's session is easier to reach than for Rogers' session.

3. There is no trainee homework, but there is homework for the group leader. After this session, compile the statistics of trainees' ratings for Rogers' and Beitman's working alliances, as well as the WAI from the trainees' and their patients' ratings of working alliance of the third sessions during pretraining. Here are the subscales of WAI and the polarity of items that you will use in your statistics. For a positive polarity (+), simply add the score; for a negative polarity (−), subtract the score from 8 and then add the result.

Scoring Key for the WAI

36 Items:

Task scale:	2, 4, 7, 11, 13, 15, 16, 18, 24, 31, 33, 35.
Polarity	+ + − − + − + + + − − +
Bond scale:	1, 5, 8, 17, 19, 20, 21, 23, 26, 28, 29, 36.
Polarity	− + + + + − + + + + − +
Goal scale:	3, 6, 9, 10, 12, 14, 22, 25, 27, 30, 32, 34.
Polarity	− + − − − + + + − + + −

12 Items: (the polarity of all items except 11 is "+")

Task scale:	1, 2, 3, 4.
Bond scale:	5, 6, 7, 8.
Goal Scale:	9, 10, 11, 12.

Session 4

Purpose: To review statistics on working alliance (Rogers, Beitman, and resident/patient ratings).

1. Following are tables describing the results of WAI ratings from several different groups from the University of Missouri. Show to your trainees the group scores of the WAI rating of the two therapists. This is intended to be a more objective rating of each therapist. You can use the data provided in Tables 2–1, 2–2, 2–3, and 2–4 to demonstrate differences between your current trainees and other groups. The groups that rated Rogers include three groups of residents (at UMC) being trained in this program and one group composed of psychiatric faculty members. Of note in the Rogers ratings is the consistency of total score across three of the four groups (Group 1 was somewhat higher than the rest; we explain this in part by the fact that Group 1 rated the working alliance as module 1 rather than module 2). Also, all groups rated Rogers highest on the "bonds" subscale. Two groups of residents and the faculty group rated Dr. Beitman's working alliance. In addition, Dr. Beitman and his patient rated the working alliance; their total scores were almost

identical. Each trainee can compare his or her own ratings of Rogers and Beitman with those of other trainees, as well as to the group averages.

UMC Residents' and Faculty's Rating of Working Alliance

TABLE 2-1   Working Alliance of Dr. Rogers' Session (36 Items)

	Group One	Group Two	Group Three	Faculty
X	218.63	192.50	197.86	187.17
SD	14.13	20.40	19.95	20.73
N	8	4	7	6

TABLE 2-2   Subscales of Dr. Rogers' Working Alliance

		Group One	Group Two	Group Three	Faculty
Task	X	71.63	59.50	66.14	57.50
	SD	4.96	8.67	8.80	7.87
Bond	X	78.00	72.75	69.86	71.33
	SD	4.2	3.78	7.29	3.01
Goals	X	69.00	57.25	61.86	56.67
	SD	7.71	11.30	8.03	12.61

TABLE 2-3   Working Alliance of Dr. Beitman's Session (36 Items)

	Group Two	Group Three	Faculty	Beitman	Patient
X	210.00	223.86	198.00	234	232
SD	7.44	11.20	20.4	20.73	
N	4	7	11		

TABLE 2-4   Subscales of Dr. Beitman's Working Alliance

		Group Two	Group Three	Faculty	Beitman	Patient
Task	X	69.75	74.43	66.60	76	80
	SD	3.00	3.82	7.10		
Bond	X	71.75	76.86	66.70	81	70
	SD	6.40	5.58	7.70		
Goals	X	68.50	72.57	64.60	77	82
	SD	3.31	4.54	6.90		

    2. How do the trainees explain the differences between the other group ratings and their own? Perhaps differences are related to how closely Rogers and Beitman matched the trainee's own style or how the rater felt about the interaction. Beitman's differences from Rogers might be explained by (1) Beitman's being closer to the current way of doing psychotherapy, i.e., he is more active; (2) Beitman's having had three sessions while Rogers was meeting Gloria for first time; (3) trainees' possible preference for Beitman because they knew him; (4) possibly the order in which tapes were rated.

During the session, you have also presented the results of trainees' ratings of the working alliance from their third session in pretraining. Differences between the patient's and therapist's rating of the same working alliance can illustrate excessive modesty or confidence. If one trainee-patient pair shares a large discrepancy, the group might begin the exercise by guessing who the trainee is. Comparing the patient's rating with the therapist's can help trainees to become aware of how patients and therapists sometimes perceive the working alliance differently. Since this perception varies with the patient, trainees will need to know which scores belong to which of their two patients. When comparing the trainee rating with Rogers/Beitman ratings, keep in mind that the trainees are using a 12-item scale while Rogers/Beitman was a 36-item scale. For example, the Rogers rating of 210 translates into a 12-item rating of 70. It should also be remembered that outside observers, therapists, and patients differ in their ratings.

From this discussion trainees gain the following:

1. They learn that as beginners they should be emphasizing bond formation.
2. They begin to see what abilities they need to develop later regarding tasks and bonds.
3. They begin to identify themselves as "bond" people or "task" people or "goal" people.
4. The numerical ratings help them to feel that they have actually done something with their patients.

Without proposing answers, we raise the question of whether a resident's own predisposition to establishing bonds, tasks, or goals influenced the way they rated. We also ask what predisposition they have now and what would they like to develop.

    3. Homework: Ask trainees to review the Exploitation Index (Form 14-1) and the Description of Exploitation Index (Form 14-2).

Session 5

Purpose: To have trainees complete COSE (Post-module 2) and GI (Post-module 2) in the first 20 minutes. In the remaining 40 minutes review the subscales of the Exploitation Index, which consists of seven subscales that explore the therapist's behaviors, thoughts, and feelings beyond the professional role. This discussion is intended to help trainees increase their awareness of boundary issues and to give them the opportunity to examine their own behaviors with regard to any particular patient. Complete the GITC after this session (see page 9).

    1. After the trainees complete COSE and GI, the group discusses the subcategories and the items on the Form 14-1 and Form 14-2. The definition of each subscale is read aloud and discussed. Each trainee should offer comments. Discussion should include delineating those items that seem too rigid and those items that

point to necessary boundaries. This discussion should help the trainees be aware of and understand boundary violations.

2. The discussions in our training included:

   a. General boundary violations. Many disagree with the stricture to not accept patient referrals from patients or friends. We recognize that these are relatively rigid requirements that occasionally may be disregarded.
   b. Eroticism. Discussion of the mechanism by which "the therapist consciously and unconsciously molds the patient into an ideal sexual partner" requires subtlety beyond most trainees' experience and usually leads to further discussion of countertransference. This topic is reserved for module 6.
   c. Exhibitionism. This serves as an example of using the patient for one's own benefit. What can a therapist talk about appropriately with a patient?
   d. Dependency. Silence and coming late are confusing examples for the residents. But they understand that some therapists will strive for heroic endurance of patient resistance in order to keep the patient feeling fully and completely accepted.
   e. Power seeking. When to direct (medications, homework, involuntary hospitalization) and when to collaborate. Some trainees recognize their desire to control and be the authority.
   f. Greediness. Because of managed care capitation of a provider group, one provider may refer to a member of the provider group rather than pay fee-for-service to someone outside the group. This illustrates the ethical dilemma of managed care, as residents may be torn between patient care and financial gain.
   g. Enabling. Trainees see the enabling therapist as one who endures all the negative responses a patient can present without drawing the line or considering termination. It is similar to dependency.

3. Homework: Ask trainees to preview module 3 text in *LP*.

MODULE 3

Inductive Reasoning to Determine Patterns

SESSIONS

Session 1

Purpose: To go through the text of module 3. You need to spend the last 15 minutes discussing the "cherry pie" case in the introduction of Form 15-1.

1. The discussion should focus on the use of inductive reasoning to define maladaptive (as well as adaptive) patterns. You can give one or two examples of the thought processes involved in pattern induction. In this module, we present three levels of patterns. First-level patterns are used most frequently by trainees to label patients' problems. However, we don't emphasize first-level patterns since trainees are often familiar with them and the patterns do not clearly delineate what patients need to change. Level-two patterns are psychotherapy school-based patterns; they are described in Appendix I. Study of these patterns helps trainees to develop their own theories of mind as they begin the lifelong exercise of sharpening their ideas about the ways human beings think and feel. However clear these models of mind are to trainees, they are useless unless they can be applied to patients in the real world of the consulting room. Level three defines patterns that suggest to both therapist and patient what needs to be done to change the pattern.

2. In our training, the discussion often begins with "What is a dysfunctional pattern?" and continues with the need to define "dysfunctional" collaboratively with the patient, recognizing that our views of good and bad, dysfunctional or functional, may not be the same as the patient's.

3. Homework: The group members review Form 15-1 (Inductive Reasoning to Determine Patterns) as they begin to learn how to build on their ability to induce patterns (e.g., diagnoses), allowing about 15 minutes. We encourage them to think like physicians. For example, if, during a physical examination, the physician detects pain over the right upper quadrant of the abdomen, he/she will pursue diagnostic possibilities related to the liver. In the same way, painful or odd or out-of-the-ordinary thoughts, feelings, and/or behaviors serve as entrées to psychological patterns. In this exercise the trainees attempt to induce general patterns from the case vignettes without discussing them with colleagues or friends.

Session 2

Purpose: To discuss Form 15-1. This session is intended to guide trainees' thinking in defining patients' patterns and to encourage them to formulate the pattern demonstrated in the vignette in terms that the patient can understand. You might also take this opportunity to demonstrate general principles of mental functioning in the vignettes.

1. The group discusses the 10 vignettes (Form 15-1) from which the trainees have already derived the patterns as homework. If some trainees have not completed the homework assignment, the group may briefly discuss the possible reasons as an illustration of the reasons patients do not do homework. The trainees report the patterns they induced to the group and explain their results. There may be disagreements, which you will encourage them to discuss. The discussion needs to be directed to the different levels of patterns. You can use the Answers to Form 16-1 to facilitate the discussion.

2. Generally, trainees grasp the idea of pattern induction, but they tend to use first-level patterns, such as "low self-esteem" and "paranoid," to describe patients. They struggle with describing the pattern to the patient. Stress the importance of studying the patterns and describing them in words that a patient could understand.

During this discussion, trainees begin to see that patients have developed maladaptive patterns for specific, future-directed reasons, which might be called the patient intentions behind the patterns (e.g., fear of rejection, fear of conflict, fear of being blamed, fear of self-expression). Defining the feared, anticipated, desired consequence becomes part of the pattern definition. We attempt to keep the discussion at the surface, staying within the limited data of each vignette. After defining the pattern, we then encourage trainees to look for unconscious conflicts, hidden motives, and triggers of old painful memories. Many simply try to order the patient to change rather than describing the pattern and implying what should be done.

3. Homework: Ask trainees to complete Form 16-1 (Transcripts for Inductive Reasoning).

Session 3

Purpose: To review Form 16-1. In this exercise trainees formulate patients' patterns from dialogues. Transcripts have more information, more closely resemble the real world, and therefore present greater challenges in detecting patterns.

1. You may want to explore several different perspectives from different schools of therapy about what is going on with these patients. Ask trainees not only to describe the pattern but also to pretend to convey it to the patient. Each trainee should have a chance to report and discuss possible patterns induced from the transcripts.

2. In our training, this discussion is intentionally loose and free-flowing in order to give trainees the opportunity to think flexibly together (a kind of antidote to *DSM-IV* categorical thinking).

3. Homework: The group goes to Form 17 (Triple-column Diary). It takes about five to ten minutes to introduce the triple-column techniques (Beck, Rush, Shaw, & Emery, 1979). The group discusses how to assign the homework to patients. Emphasize that the therapist needs to help patients understand that it is their responsibility to do the homework. You should mention how to deal with possible patient reactions. For example, patients might refuse to do the homework. What are some possible reasons? Therapists must avoid criticizing patients and instead explore with them reasons for not doing the homework. This may form another inducing point.

We recommend that for the next week trainees use the triple-column dairy to write down their own feelings (e.g., excessive anger), unwanted thoughts (e.g., excessive self-criticism), or maladaptive behavior (e.g., smoking) associated with specific events.

Session 4

Purpose: To review Form 17. We ask trainees to use the triple-column diary themselves, rather than with their patients, for the following reasons: (1) The triple-column technique is a structured homework exercise that promotes ongoing self-observation in patients who agree to do it. This exercise provides one of several ways to teach patients how to self-observe. By doing this exercise, trainees learn the details of this technique; then they can teach their patients how to use this diary correctly. (2) One of the goals of this training program is to stimulate trainees' observing self. The triple-column exercise helps trainees develop their ability to observe their thinking and feeling about themselves in the role of therapist as they process information from patients. By studying their own inductive reasoning thought processes, trainees refine their ability to monitor and direct their thinking.

1. The trainees discuss their triple-column diaries with the group and attempt to articulate their personal patterns.

2. Trainees report that, by doing this homework, they become aware of automatic thoughts. One trainee defined a pattern of excessive self-doubt (he was late twice to meetings and was rejected by a patient for being a trainee) and recorded his automatic thoughts of self-criticism and fear of being punished by others. Another described angry arguments with his wife around money and realized through the diary how each of them was bringing different attitudes toward money from their families of origin. Another became angry and frightened about a violent patient and recorded his automatic thoughts, realizing how truly "automatic" they were. Another reported becoming very anxious about his elderly father in another country dying at the birth of his second child. The diary helped him see that this was related to the fact that his mother had died on the birthday of his first child.

Discussion of such issues leads to further attempts by trainees to see underlying schemas. For example, one trainee became excessively angry when patients did not inform him of their decisions to change medication or when administrators did not treat patients correctly. His excessive anger was related to his feeling of "being ignored." The trainees in the group related that to his "need for control" and possibly to his fear of "being abandoned." The trainee accepted the first idea but denied the relevance of the second. He began to see the outline of his conflict and underlying distorted schema.

Session 5

Purpose: To review two videotape vignettes from patients treated by Beitman. Require them to use the second-level patterns associated with the different schools of psychotherapy to define "well-formed" patterns.

   1. The group members watch segments of Beitman's sessions with MC and MF and discuss the patients' patterns.

   Before the group watches the tape, present the following information about the patients: MC is a "Southern Belle" with generalized anxiety disorder, treated with low doses of Effexor, who has trouble saying "no." (This session is also used in module 4 as a demonstration of interpersonal strategies for change.) MF is a 48-year-old woman with panic disorder and an odd form of agoraphobia. Rather than being confined to her house, she must at times leave because of high anxiety. The segment describes her struggles with her husband and her fear of expressing her needs to him. (This third session from MF was used as a transcript in module 1 and as a videotape to be rated for working alliance in module 2.) You may use tapes from your own faculty that illustrate problematic patterns being defined during the session.

   Trainees are asked to describe the patients' patterns. They should be encouraged to clarify specific inducing points. Most trainees can filter information on their own and identify patients' patterns. They tend to describe general patterns, such as "the patient has low self-esteem." Encourage them to refine those patterns until they develop suggestions about how to change.

   2. Trainees struggle with the complexity of the association between fear, anger, and anxiety. They are able to try different school-based formulas for packaging the pattern. For the vignette with MC, most trainees can identify with her need to please and can generate several alternative descriptions of the pattern using past-present, automatic thoughts, interpersonal schemas, etc. The discussion usually yields some interesting questions about how therapists make value judgments based on underlying cultural assumptions about normal and abnormal behavior.

   3. Homework: Ask trainees to complete Form 15-2 (Inductive Reasoning to Determine Patterns).

Session 6 (Optional)

Because perceiving patterns from videotapes requires careful assimilation of information, an additional videotape presentation and discussion may be provided. Our experience has been that trainees learn well from videotape analysis. If your site has an additional videotape, it can be used during this session.

Session 7

Purpose: To review Form 15-2 case vignettes from which trainees have induced patterns. Form 15-2 is similar to Form 15-1. We repeat this exercise format to help solidify trainees' knowledge base.

   1. You can use Answers to Form 15-2 to facilitate the discussion, which should involve trainees' interacting, questioning, and responding to each other more than with Form 15-1.

   2. You may notice the differences between trainees' answers to Form 15-1 and Form 15-2. With our trainees we have seen some remarkable transformations.

Suddenly they can see the possibility of patterns other than *DSM-IV* diagnoses. Their minds are open to ideas from different schools not only in the case vignettes but also in their work settings.

    3. Homework: Ask trainees to complete Form 16-2 (Transcripts for Inductive Reasoning).

Session 8

Purpose: To have trainees complete COSE (Post-module 3) and Guided Inquiry (Post-module 3) during the first 20 minutes and to review Form 16-2 for patterns from two different transcripts. You need to complete GITC after this session (see page 9).

    1. After trainees complete COSE and GI, the group discusses Form 16-2, which follows the same format as Form 16-1. You can use Answers to Form 16-2 to facilitate the discussion.

    2. The first transcript, which involves a patient of Albert Ellis, can lead to a discussion of freedom and responsibility as well as clarification of the differences between cognitive schema and automatic thoughts. How much did the patient's growing up and leaving home influence the increasing alcoholism of her father?

    The second transcript shows a borderline/narcissistic patient interacting with the therapist. It stirs up countertransference and permits discussion of weak self/other boundaries, grandiose and depreciated self.

    3. Homework: Ask trainees to preview module 4 text in *LP*.

SUGGESTED ANSWERS TO FORM 15-1

1. She cannot accept anything positive about herself. (Disqualifying the positive)
   She does not trust men.
2. He held himself responsible for problems he did not create. (Personalizing)
3. She gives "love" and she wants to be appreciated but she cannot ask directly. (Sacrifices herself in order to get love of others)
4. She is afraid of somebody criticizing her for not being enthusiastic and warm. (Overly dependent on the opinion of others)
   She fears losing friends. (Fear of isolation)
5. He tries to avoid the fights by agreeing with her. He is afraid of confronting the marital problems. (Avoid interpersonal conflicts)
   He thought quarreling with his wife would lead to losing her. (Fear of low probability events)
6. He needed to control his wife; he felt threatened if he could not. (If someone disagrees with him, he feels threatened.)
7. No matter how hard she tries she believes she will never do the task right. (She cannot live up to her own expectations and believes others hold her to the same very high standards.)
8. The patient arbitrarily concluded that people will not negotiate with him. (Jumping to conclusions)
9. Her pattern: blame him entirely for events to which she contributed a part. (Blame others, do not accept blame)
   His pattern: to accept the blame entirely without insisting that they both contributed. ("Everything bad is my fault.")
   The couple patterns: she blames him for all problems between them; he accepts the blame.
   (One takes too much responsibility, the other takes too little.)
10. She feared that she was not competent anymore because of the brain injury and that her colleagues would find out and she would lose her job. (Excessive fear of failure based upon a real possibility)
11. Similar to the way she reacted to the death of her dog. She became acutely anxious and distressed. (Exquisitely sensitive to interpersonal loss)
12. No matter how hard she tries, no one will care about her. Those who clearly do not care about her can become objects of hate. (Terrified by and furious at those who abandon her)

SUGGESTED ANSWERS TO FORM 16-1

Case 1.

The patient's possible patterns:

1. She perceives things with "all or nothing" or "white or black" attitude.
2. She can't accept positive or good feelings about herself.
3. She anticipates the bad feeling after the good feeling.
4. She believes other people can be helped but not her.
5. She can't maintain a relationship with a man but she needs a man to be happy.
6. She is content when in a relationship with man, but feels depression when by herself.

Case 2.

Rachel's possible patterns:

1. She behaves like a boy to please her father and tries to comfort him.
2. She thinks she is the one who takes care of and comforts her father in this family.
3. She takes too much responsibility for her father.

Mother's possible patterns:

1. When she feels lonely or needs somebody to be nice to her, she will go back to her parents.
2. Nobody except Sandy in this family really takes care of me.
3. I go back to my parents because they are old and need me.
4. She thinks her husband needs Rachel to take care of him rather than a wife.
5. She feels rejected by rest of family and allows Rachel to take over caring for her husband.

Father's possible patterns:

1. He complains of his wife being too close to her family.
2. He pays more attention to Rachel than to his wife.
3. The fact that he is not in the interview may be significant. He may be content with the current situation.

Possible patterns between Rachel and father:

1. Rachel tries to please him by being like a boy, but she is not successful enough.
2. Rachel plays two roles with her father: One is father's boy, the other is a nurturing pseudo wife.
3. Father likes Rachel's boy personality and becomes accustomed to her caring about him.

Possible patterns between Rachel and mother:

1. Rachel doesn't believe her mother can take care of her father.
2. Mother doesn't like her daughter's boyish characters.

Possible patterns between the mother and father:

1. She blames him for not taking care of her.
2. He blames her for choosing her parents over him.

Possible pattern among Rachel, father and mother:

1. Mother complains that her husband doesn't care about her and doesn't need a wife because he pays more attention to Rachel than to her. Rachel can take care of her father as a daughter and please him by acting like a boy. By going back to her parents for comfort rather than turning to her husband, mother allows Rachel and her father to maintain their alliance.

SUGGESTED ANSWERS TO FORM 15-2

1. She could not accept that her mother treated both of them equally. (Disqualifying the positive)
2. He preferred to tough it out rather than correct the difficulties. (Persistently avoids confronting difficulties)
3. It is hard for her to say "No" to somebody else's requests. (Other people's needs and wishes are more important than her own.)
4. She must feel superior to other women or else she cannot develop a relationship with them. (Win or leave)
5. If things are not just as they should be, he is a failure. (Tyranny of the "shoulds")
6. She thinks that nothing could help, no matter what she does. (Lack of belief in her own ability to effect a better future)
7. He abuses her with his drinking. He becomes sober and apologizes when she threatens to leave. She does not leave. (Whatever he does, she accepts.)
8. People in authority over her will ignore her needs. (No one cares about me.)
9. She inhibited herself from any sexually suggestive conduct with a man because the man might think she was promiscuous and would leave her. (Excessive sense of influence over the behavior of others)
10. If the person with whom he is involved withdraws emotionally, he feels threatened with possible abandonment. (Excessive fear of abandonment by person for whom he cares)
11. She expects her roommates to anticipate her needs and respond to them whenever she wants. (Wants others to take care of her needs without having to ask)

SUGGESTED ANSWERS TO FORM 16-2

Case 1:

1. If she doesn't do what her parents ask her to do, she will feel guilty.
2. It is wrong if she thinks of herself.
3. Everything her parents say is right, and she hasn't been able to stop believing this.
4. She fears being rejected by other people, which might relate to the fear of being rejected by her parents.
5. She can't write fiction because she fears that she couldn't do it very well because her family insisted that she couldn't do well in school.
6. She is promiscuous because she thinks this is the only way to be valued, loved, approved of by a man.
7. Summary statements of problem patterns: Whatever I do will not work out successfully; I am better off not trying to do well at school, work, or relationships. (I therefore must stay home with my parents and do as they say. If I am successful and leave home, I will feel guilty about my parents.)
Restated: Since I cannot be successful in the world, I must stay home and take care of my parents who need me. I feel guilty for having thoughts of leaving.

Case 2:

1. She blames her husband and refuses to take responsibility for their marital difficulties.
2. Her feelings of self-worth depend on her husband's (or other persons') reactions to her.
3. She feels both entitled and worthless.
4. The simultaneous existence of an entitled, powerful, demanding aspect together with a helpless and worthless aspect.

MODULE 4

Strategies for Change

SESSIONS

Session 1

Purpose: To review text of Module 4 in *LP*. This presents the complexities of the process of change, emphasizing the basic sequence of identifying a pattern, giving it up, initiating a new pattern, and maintaining it. Trainees are offered a list of generic change processes (Appendix II) and a longer list of change processes associated with the different schools of psychotherapy (Appendix III). Here they become acquainted in a highly condensed way with the major approaches to helping people change.

1. Go through the module 4 text with the group. There are many details to trigger discussion. The most complicated elements involve the two figures, the table, and the two glossaries. It will take two sessions to go through the text. We suggest that the discussion in this session focus on the three substages of change, three orders of change, generic strategies for change, and the interaction of ECBIS as implied in Figure 4–2. The next session is used to discuss ECBIS strategies for change.

2. There is a very strong connection between modules 3 and 4. The discussion of patients' patterns in the previous module prepares trainees to learn the strategies and techniques. Trainees are also excited to enter this module because they anticipate that it will provide them the tools for psychotherapy.

In their different ways, trainees begin to grasp details of the process of change. Seeing change as less mysterious, as well as partially beyond their influence, they become clearer about the process and more humble about their contribution.

3. Homework: Ask trainees to read Appendix II (Generic strategies and techniques) and Appendix III (ECBIS strategies and techniques).

Session 2

Purpose: To continue to discuss the text and review the ECBIS glossary.

1. Appendix III describes the strategies listed in Table 4–1. The group should go through them together. Start by asking some questions about these readings. The discussion will focus on strategies that trainees have trouble understanding.

2. Trainees are exposed to various approaches from different psychotherapy schools. We try both to enhance their comfort with ones they already use and to broaden their range of choices. It is valuable for trainees to notice how they differ among themselves in their predispositions toward the various approaches.

3. Homework: Spend about five minutes demonstrating how to do Form 18-1 (Transcripts for Change Strategies).

Session 3

Purpose: To review Form 18-1. As they attempt to recognize the strategies used in transcripts, trainees have to go back to ECBIS glossary and carefully consider the meaning of various strategies and techniques. Form 18-1 also provides a view of how these strategies are used by different psychotherapists.

1. The group members discuss Form 18-1, reporting their answers. Focus on the substage(s) of change as well as generic and specific strategies and techniques. You should also provide guidance about the ECBIS strategies and techniques that appear in that transcript, while recognizing that many of the labels for strategies and techniques overlap. While doing this, help trainees to become aware of the relationships between change substages, between the generic and specific strategies, and among the ECBIS strategies and techniques. Use Answers to Form 18-1 to facilitate your discussion.

It may not be possible to discuss all ten transcripts in an hour. We have found that psychotherapy supervisors perform two key functions for modules 3 and 4: (1) go over the definitions in the glossaries and (2) review trainee answers to the homework not discussed.

2. Generally, the discussion helps trainees identify, clarify, and discriminate among some confusing strategies.

From the first transcript of Minuchin's case, our trainees see how changes in a father might bring about change in a daughter and mother (systems thinking) and how this system orientation differs from an intrapsychic one. Discussion of the second transcript from Greenberg leads to understanding empathic reflections and how they can aid in changing thinking by focusing on emotion. The third transcript from Basch provokes discussion of the substages of change. They have difficulty seeing that change has taken place and that this session is helping to maintain it. Instead they believe that change is being initiated in this session.

Some trainees study the glossaries enthusiastically because they believe that finally they have come to the keys to doing psychotherapy. While they generally recognize the value of the previous modules, they find these strategies and techniques particularly appealing due to their usefulness.

3. Homework: Ask trainees to complete Form 19-1 (Case Vignettes for Change Strategies). Spend about ten minutes discussing the example in Form 19-1 in which trainees are asked to consider which strategies or techniques the therapist might use.

Session 4

Purpose: To review Form 19-1. This homework gives trainees an opportunity to try out the various strategies in a group discussion. The exercise intends to broaden trainees' thinking and choices in dealing with any given patient.

1. Trainees are asked to report generic and ECBIS strategies for each case. Answers to Form 19-1 may help you to facilitate the discussion. You can start with generic strategies and then move on to ECBIS strategies. Encourage trainees to try to think "how to help this identified patient from different approaches," rather than to evaluate which strategy best fits the patient.

2. Trainees' answers often reflect their personal orientations. They can widen their choice of strategies by listening to other trainees justify their selections.

Trainees find these two cases quite time-consuming because there is much to review and to consider. The first case involves a young woman who wants to be taken care of by her roommates and her therapist. They find it easier than the second, which involves a teacher with a brain injury after an auto accident. They do not know how to deal with her injury—how significant is it and how much is she exaggerating her disability? Instead of inquiring about evidence to substantiate this question, some trainees simply assume that she is brain-injured and may have to consider retirement.

Session 5

Purpose: To review and discuss brief videotape vignettes demonstrating strategies focusing on emotion (E), cognition (C), behavior (B), interpersonal (I), and system (S). These tapes give trainees the chance to discuss ECBIS techniques as well as to see different therapists in action. Watching videotapes gives trainees various models to "try on" for themselves.

We suggest that you use two sessions to review these vignettes.* Generally, we review E, C, and B in session 5 and I and S in session 6. While each vignette could be discussed in greater detail, our purpose here is to seed trainees with visual-experiential images of ECBIS categories.

1. Before the group watches each vignette, ask trainees to read its short introduction in *LP* (page 151). Remind trainees to pay attention to the underlined strategies and techniques. Direct the discussion to focus on the substages of changes, comparing ECBIS strategies, emphasizing the similarity and differences of ECBIS strategies, and helping trainees clarify the strategies as specifically as possible.

2. Trainees appreciate seeing the direct application of what they have read. They are often curious about whether these are actors or real patients. (The answer depends upon which vignettes you have purchased or developed.) They have the most trouble grasping the empty chair technique of gestalt therapy (and it is the most complicated). They make interesting comparisons among the therapists, commenting on degrees of support: empathy, encouragement, praise, remembering to ask about the homework you assigned. They note that gestalt therapy stays within the session and that behavior therapy is focused on what goes on outside the session.

---

* Videotapes may be ordered from the following:
(1) Greenberg, Person, and Kaslow tapes from the American Psychological Association Psychotherapy Series I: 1-800-374-2721.
(2) Mirris from Annenberg: 1-800-LEARNER (532-7637).
(3) Beitman from W. W. Norton (companion videotage to *Learning Psychotherapy*): 1-800-233-4830.

Session 6

Purpose: To review interpersonal and system videotape vignettes.

    1. The procedure is same as the previous session.

    2. In our training, the discussion usually centers around the following questions: Should this interpersonal vignette have been placed under interpersonal or should it have been cognitive or behavioral? What is the difference between behavioral role-playing and emotion-focused empty chair? How does systems thinking build upon interpersonal, which builds upon cognitive-emotional-behavioral?

    3. Homework: Ask trainees to complete Form 18-2 (Transcripts for Change Strategies).

Session 7

Purpose: To review Form 18-2, which has a format similar to Form 18-1.

    1. The procedure is same as session 3. You can use Answers to Form 18-2 to facilitate the discussion.

    2. Trainees continue to struggle with the relationships between and among these five ways of conceptualizing psychological functioning. They begin to see that emotion, cognition, and behavior make up the interpersonal and that the interpersonal makes up systems. They begin to realize that changes in cognition can influence interpersonal relationships, that changes in interpersonal relationships can influence systems, and that change in systems can influence change in behavior.

    3. Homework: Ask trainees to complete Form 19-2 (Case Vignettes for Change Strategies).

Session 8

Purpose: To have trainees complete COSE and GI (the first 20 minutes), and to review Form 19-2 (the remaining 40 minutes). Complete GITC after the session (see page 9).

    After trainees complete COSE (Post-module 4) and (Post-module 4), they discuss Form 19-2. The procedure for this session is same as session 4. Use Answers to Form 19-2 to facilitate the discussion.

    Homework: Ask trainees to preview module 5 text in *LP*.

ANSWERS TO FORM 18-1

I	1. a	2. d	
II	1. b	2. c	
III	1. d	2. c	3. c
IV	1. a	2. b	
V	1. b	2. a	3. a
VI	1. a	2. d	3. b
VII	1. d	2. d	
VIII	1. b	2. a	

SUGGESTED ANSWERS TO FORM 19-1

Case 1:

1. The generic strategies and techniques the therapist might use:
   - Define the dysfunctional pattern
   - Decide what to change
   - Take responsibility (such as the responsibility for taking care of herself and the responsibility for change)
   - Self-disclosure (the therapist can help the patient understand why her roommates left her by talking about his own feelings or reactions to the patient's behaviors toward him)
   - Separate past from present (for example, the patient's interpersonal scripts may reflect the patterns with her parents)
2. The ECBIS strategies and techniques might be:

E:

Evoking the emotion in the session:

a. Enactment of the patient's feeling when her roommates did not "take care of her" while she was sick.
b. Help her reexperience the feared reactions when others did not respond to her in a way she needed.

Restructuring emotional schemas:

a. Help the patient access new information through emotional awareness by detailed re-experiencing of situation of being sick and being ignored by roommates.
b. Reconceptualize the patient's internal experience by defining more appropriate emotional responses.
c. Confront feared emotion of being abandoned, neglected.

Maintaining the reorganized emotion schemas:

The therapist can reinforce the patient's new emotional reaction to the same situation.

C:

Identifying and challenging the distorted beliefs:

The therapist helps the patient define the distorted belief "nobody cared about me" by reality-testing and questioning the evidence.

Creating adaptive and reasonable beliefs:

The therapist challenges the patient's distorted belief by reattribution, developing alternatives and disputing irrational thinking.

Repeating and practicing the modified belief in a variety of situations:

The therapist continues to discuss the patient's new thinking when she is in related situations and reinforces these new thoughts.

I:

Identifying maladaptive interpersonal schemas:

a. Analyze the patient's scenarios by demonstrating how the patient repeats with the therapist patterns from her relationship with her roommates.
b. Examine the patient's interpersonal pull by being both a participant and observer (the therapist can help the patient understand others' reaction to her by discussing her pull in the here-and-now relationship; the therapist is likely to be "pulled" to rescue the patient).

Modifying and altering interpersonal scripts:

a. Provide new and constructive interpersonal experiences by using the here-and-now therapeutic relationship to show concern without rescuing.
b. Help the patient to rewrite, modify, and correct the assumptions underlying her scenarios (for example, help her become aware that her roommate doesn't have the responsibility for anticipating her needs and responding to them without being asked, and that her roommate's inattentiveness doesn't mean that nobody cares about her).

Practice modified roles:

Practice and reinforce new interpersonal successes that involve not trying to induce others to do for herself what she can do.

Case 2

1. Generic strategies and techniques that might be used:
   - Define dysfunctional patterns related to excessive fears of criticism
   - Challenge dysfunctional belief and emotion (such as "I am not competent anymore and my colleagues will find out")
   - Decide what to change (quit teaching? more rehabilitation? change thinking?)
   - Face fear of failure (so what if I fail?)
   - Role play herself and other teachers' reactions to her
2. ECBIS strategies and techniques that might be used:

E:

Evoking her fear of being criticized by role-playing in order to activate her fears.

Restructuring her emotional schema:

a. Help the patient reconceptualize internal experience through role-play of being afraid of failure and criticism.
b. Confront thoughts and relationship consequences of losing her job.

C:

Identifying and challenging her dysfunctional belief (she is not competent anymore):

a. Question the evidence for her incompetence after the brain injury. It is very possible that the patient felt incompetent because of her excessive fear rather than brain injury.
b. Test reality (Do her colleagues find her incompetent? How bad must she be to lose her job?)

Creating reasonable belief by allowing new information to enter information-processing:

a. Develop alternatives (help the patient think about other possible explanations for her "incompetence").
b. Fantasize consequences (what will happen if her colleagues find out she is now incompetent?).
c. Dispute irrational belief that she is incompetent.

Practice:

Change self-talk (such as change "I am not competent anymore and my colleagues will find out and I will lose my job" to "My incompetent feeling comes from my excessive fear rather than reality" and "I am still competent for my job since I have handled it very well for so many years").

B:

Identifying maladaptive behaviors:

Self-monitoring of errors in teaching and lesson planning.

Changing behavior directly:

a. Relaxation training to be used when beginning to feel anxious.
b. Systematic desensitization (construct and face fear hierarchy of levels of criticism and levels of failure).

Practice modified behaviors:

a. Use relaxation training outside of teaching (e.g., with anger-provoking children).
b. Learn to face fears of job loss and other potential failures.

I:

Identifying maladaptive interpersonal schemas:

a. Interpretation: With sufficient information, demonstrate relationship between current self-doubt and family of origin upbringing.
b. Identify interpersonal patterns within therapeutic relationship: The patient may suspect that the therapist will criticize her for the way she fills the role of patient (e.g., asking for additional medications).

Modifying role relationship models and altering interpersonal scripts:

Helping modify assumptions underlying interpersonal scripts. She may believe "If I am not competent as a teacher, no one will like me and I will not like myself," or "I am now handicapped. I dislike anyone who does not do her job, so no one really wants to work with me or support me."

Practice modified roles and patterns:

Reinforcement from new interpersonal success: The therapist can interpret the meaning of positive change—"You have worked hard to demonstrate to yourself that you are competent. You are selecting the positive evidence and you can keep doing that."

S:

Spouse and family data not given.

ANSWERS TO FORM 18-2

I	1. a	2. a
II	1. d	2. d
III	1. a	2. a
IV	1. b	2. b
V	1. c	2. a
VI	1. c	2. a
VII	1. b	2. b
VIII	1. a	2. d
IX	1. c	2. c

SUGGESTED ANSWERS TO FORM 19-2

Case 1

1. Generic strategies and techniques that should be used with this patient:
   - Defining the dysfunctional pattern (he arbitrarily concludes that people will not negotiate with him—jumping to conclusion)
   - Challenging the dysfunctional belief ("How do you know I would be angry?")
   - Deciding to change his belief that others will not respond to his needs
   - Alter future expectation of people's response to his needs
   - Face fear of bringing up his needs or fear of being refused
   - Practice new assertiveness
2. The ECBIS strategies and techniques for this patient:

E:

Evoke emotion in the session:

Evoking the patient's emotion by enacting the real situations (such as talking about the immediate feelings when the patient didn't ask for the more convenient time, or the same feelings in similar situations).

Restructuring an emotional schema:

a. Helping the patient to access new information through emotional awareness (help the patient to be aware of his irrational fear of being ignored and refused).
b. Reconceptualizing his internal experience by helping him understand his emotional schema.

C:

Identifying and challenging his dysfunctional belief:

Questioning the evidence and testing the reality for his dysfunctional belief (for this patient, the therapist questions the evidence for his belief that his demands are always ignored or refused. The therapist tries to help the patient find the evidence that shows that some people really care about his needs).

Creating reasonable belief by allowing new information that is discrepant with the previous belief to enter information-processing:

a. Developing alternatives (help the patient find alternative explanation when people don't negotiate with him).
b. Fantasizing consequences (help the patient imagine what would happen if he were to bring up his needs and people wouldn't negotiate with him).
c. Disputing irrational beliefs: "What do I (the therapist) get out of ignoring your request?"

Repeat or practice the modified belief:

Change self-talk (The patient might develop self-talk, such as "Since I can't know what other people's reactions will be until I bring up my needs, I won't conclude beforehand that they will neglect my needs." "If people don't want to negotiate with me, they may have reasons that are not necessarily related to me").

B:

Defining maladaptive behaviors:

Behavioral observation by the therapist: Note other instances when the patient avoids acting on his own behalf with the therapist.

Changing behavior directly:

Self-reinforcement: Patient rewards himself when asking for what he needs.

Practice modified behaviors in various situations:

Keep trying new assertiveness.

I:

Identifying maladaptive interpersonal schemas:

Cyclical psychodynamics: Discover that the patient ignores his needs as he induces others to ignore them.

Modifying role relationship models:

Corrective emotional experiences: The therapist responds graciously to the patient's needs.

Practice modified roles:

The therapist repeatedly responds graciously to the patient's needs.

S:

No significant other described.

Case 2

1. Generic strategies and techniques to be used with this patient:
   - Defining the dysfunctional interactive patterns in this couple
   - Deciding what to change
   - Taking responsibility (especially the wife, take the responsibility for problems between them and the responsibility for changing the pattern between them)
   - Suggesting how to change (the therapist can make several specific suggestions of how to change reacting to each other)
   - Face fear (especially for the husband, fear confronting his wife's blaming him)
   - Practice (practice the new reacting pattern between them)
2. ECBIS strategies and techniques to be used for this patient:

E:

Evoking emotion in the session:

Enactment of conflict splits—two chairs: Have him play two parts talking to each other—his strict self-punishing restrictive self dialogues with his more hidden angry, resentful self-asking, "What makes you so rigid?"

Restructuring emotional schemas:

Confronting feared emotions: Help him experience his fear of being assertive.

C:

Identifying and challenging dysfunctional beliefs:

Understanding idiosyncratic meaning: For this patient taking responsibility means being responsible for anything that goes wrong.

Creating adaptive and reasonable beliefs:

Listing positives and negatives of change: List consequences of insisting that his wife be more responsible for what happens between them (e.g., divorce vs. more loving relationship).

B:

Defining maladaptive behavior:

Self-monitoring: List all instances where wife blames him for situations in which she has at least 50% of the responsibility.

Changing behavior directly:

Assertion training: Learn how to identify and dispute situations in which she blames him excessively.

I:

Identify maladaptive interpersonal schemas:

Therapist helps patient to become aware of his pattern of always accepting his wife's blame and never challenging and confronting her blaming. If his wife joins the therapy, her dysfunctional pattern is that she always blames him rather than take her responsibility for what happened.

Modify role relationship models and alter interpersonal scripts:

Their interpersonal role disputes involve proper distribution of responsibility.

S:

Identifying the dysfunctional dynamic interactions between the spouses:

a. Circular questioning.
b. Enactment of real interactive situations in the session.

Changing interaction patterns:

a. Creating new structures by altering interactions.
b. Task-setting between the spouses.

Maintaining the new interactive pattern

Initiate and maintain a virtuous cycle (such as less blaming of the wife leads to more confidence in the husband leads to less blaming, etc.).

MODULE 5

Resistance

SESSIONS

Session 1

Purpose: To go through the text of module 5 in *LP*. Here trainees discover the common but often overlooked tendency of human beings to prevent themselves from doing what is in their own best interest.

1. The discussion will focus on the concept of resistance—its sources, forms, and management. The four tables in the text provide a good summary of the content.

2. Trainees recognize resistance from their clinical experiences and are likely to bring up their own cases. The labels and sources help them to define resistance more quickly than before. The discussion of sources also broadens trainees' thinking in analyzing the resistance. Generally, trainees start to become aware that exploring resistance also requires therapist self-examination (such as, does my inappropriate technique, or my own countertransference, contribute to the patient's resistance?). They also encounter the idea that resistance can provide an "inducing point" for general patterns of dysfunction. (One trainee who did not finish her homework several times was asked whether she had trouble completing assignments in other situations. This brought home the possibility that incidents of resistance in the present can illustrate key patterns.)

3. Homework: Ask trainees to review Form 20 (Resistance Case Vignettes).

Session 2

Purpose: To review Form 20. This exercise helps trainees understand and identify signs and sources of resistance and to think about possible ways to manage it. While discussing Form 20, you can also help them to clarify and reinforce some concepts in the text.

1. You can ask one trainee to read each case vignette. Then the trainees report their answers. There are often disagreements among trainees; you can use those as

an opportunity to clarify concepts. The group may use Table 5.4 as a reference, and Answers to Form 20 can be used to facilitate the discussion.

2. Trainees sometimes have a hard time understanding case IV because it challenges them to use the definition of resistance as a block in carrying out reasonable expectations of the patient during therapy. Several have described the source of resistance as "forces from the patient's social network," when the patient is repeating a dysfunctional pattern during the session.

Case V brings out countertransference about "saving the marriage" versus helping an individual change. There is insufficient evidence that the husband is impeding change. He might be but we don't know. In case VII, one trainee in our program had trouble labeling the reaction as transference because it seemed to be more like prejudice, which she thought to be a "lack of information." The connection between prejudice and transference lies in generalization from a small bit of information to a stereotyped view of another.

3. Homework: Ask trainees to complete Form 21 (Resistance Case Vignettes).

Session 3

Purpose: To have trainees complete COSE and GI (the first 20 minutes) and to review answers to Form 21. This homework enables them to see more clearly the forms, sources, and responses to resistance. You need to complete GITC after this session (see page 9)

1. After trainees complete COSE (Post-module 5) and (Post-module 5), they discuss Form 21, reporting their answers and discussing disagreements. Direct the discussion so that they focus on the sources, forms, and management of resistance. Ask trainees to give their answers to each question. Note differences between the Answers to Form 21 and the trainees' answers. Use vignettes where there are discrepanices for discussion.

2. Case II raises questions about the need to systematically expose the person to a feared stimulus. The data do not suggest anything other than too quick exposure, although trainees offer many other reasonable possibilities. Case VII raises the question of pessimism about change vs. pattern being demonstrated; the data are closer to pattern being demonstrated. All cases bring home the need to start with the information available. Trainees tended to infer more possibilities than are actually present. "Look at the moss on the tree, not for the whole forest, because we do not yet know if this tree is in a forest or in someone's backyard."

3. Homework: Ask trainees to preview the text of module 6 in *LP* before the next session.

ANSWERS TO FORM 20

I	1. d	2. c
II	1. a	2. c
III	1. c	2. b
IV	1. c	2. c
V	1. b	2. c
VI	1. c	2. b
VII	1. d	2. c

ANSWERS TO FORM 21

I	1. c	2. b
II	1. a	2. b
III	1. b	2. d
IV	1. b	2. b
V	1. b	2. a
VI	1. b	2. c
VII	1. c	2. d
VIII	1. d	

MODULE 6

Transference and Countertransference

SESSIONS

Session 1

Purpose: To review the text of module 6 in *LP*. It will take two sessions to go through this text. The major goals of this module are: (1) to help them see the universality of transference distortions, and (2) to help them recognize their own exaggerated and distorted reactions to their patients and to others as well.

1. You can start with questions about their reading of module 6 text. Help trainees understand the concepts of transference and countertransference and to discriminate their sources.

2. Trainees come up with various kinds of questions about transference and countertransference, such as: What is "the interactive countertransference"? If resistance takes place only within therapy relationship, is that true of transference? What triggers transference? (Ideas developed from past experiences are triggered by stimuli from the therapist. The therapist's "stimulus value" strongly influences the kinds of memories, ideas about relationships, and role relationship models that arise. For example, as a stimulus a pregnant resident evokes role expectations different from those evoked when she is not pregnant.) One trainee described a therapist who needed to be needed and seemed to use her patients as substitutes for the social network she had not developed. The point here is that *therapists are more like patients than we like to think.*

Other common questions include: How can the therapist be empathic without stimulating too much transference (like too much dependence)? How can the therapist be empathic without developing too much countertransference? (Some empathy is necessary to help establish the working alliance. The problem for some therapists is that they cannot stop from joining into the patient's experience—they identify with or become continuously involved with the patient's feeling states. The sign of maturity in a therapist is not whether one can be fully empathic or stand back to observe more objectively but rather whether one can move easily between these two perspectives.)

3. Homework: Ask trainees to review the rest of the text of module 6.

Session 2

Purpose: To continue to review the introductory text of module 6. This session focuses on the signs of transference and countertransference, nontransferential and noncountertransferential reactions, the use of transference and countertransference, and their management.

1. As in the previous session, encourage trainees to ask questions about the reading. The discussion of signs of TX and CTX should focus on helping trainees recognize them quickly once they occur in psychotherapy. In the discussion of nontransferential and noncountertransferential reactions, you can encourage them to think about how to distinguish these reactions from TX and CTX. We emphasize the importance of the observing self in the management both TX and CTX. This discussion offers another opportunity to activate each trainee's observing self, increase their willingness to self-observe, and enhance the observing self's functioning.

2. Encourage trainees to make connections between what they have learned in the seminars and what happens in clinical work. In our discussion of signs of countertransference, one trainee described excessive pity as a hindrance to being objective. Another described her lack of sympathy for chronic pain patients. Trainees learn that if their reactions are excessive or do not fit the situation, they must ask, "How much is from me and how much is from the patient?" CTX may also enter into pharmacotherapy management. In one group, a continuum of responses developed to the general question of whether or not to support the prescription of benzodiazepines.

Trainees recognize that experience helps them determine whether their reactions are CTX or not. They have yet to learn the limits of their reactions to patients. For example, excessive sympathy for a 100-year-old man who said, "I do not think I will leave the hospital," paralyzed one trainee until he realized he felt some hope and began to express it. With experience, he noted that he could still feel sympathy but more quickly pull himself back in order to offer a constructive response.

3. Homework: Continue reading module 6 text.

Session 3

Purpose: To teach CCRT method so that trainees will have a practical technique for analyzing the patient's transference.

1. The group goes to Form 22 (Standard CCRT Category) and Form 24 (Relationship Episodes). You may need 10 minutes to present the following information about CCRT.

CCRT (Core Conflict Relationship Theme) is a method to evaluate patients' relationship patterns. The basic assumption of CCRT is that any relationship interaction has three components: what the patient wants from another person, how that person reacts, and how the patient reacts to the reaction. Therapists can use these three components to analyze the patient's relationship patterns and transference.

Using CCRT, therapists need to define the relationship episodes (RE) first. RE can be defined as an explicit narration about the relationship with others or with oneself. In each RE, a person with whom the patient is interacting is identified. The second step includes identifying the three components—W: wishes, needs and intentions; RO: response from others (including the therapist); RS: response of self—in these relationship episodes. The occurrences of particular categories of W, RO, RS are counted to come up with a rating. The rater searches for a theme or themes that cross REs and apply to most of them. These themes are used to formulate the CCRT. We are not trying to train them how to define the RE and how to count the frequency; rather, we want them to learn the thought process in CCRT and the response categories so that they will better understand the components of transference and countertransference. (For more information on CCRT, see Luborsky and Crits-Christoph, 1990.)

We suggest that the group go through each response listed in Form 22 and discuss ambiguities first. The group then uses Form 23 to practice applying the response categories using their own words.

2. Trainees learn categories of responses from Form 22. Knowing these categories can help them label the patients' interpersonal patterns more readily. During the discussion of Form 23, trainees struggle with using their own words to label responses. You may need to encourage them to use their own words to describe the patients' responses and then go back to Form 22 for the standard categories. Form 23 also demonstrates how to do the homework of Form 24.

Our discussion also includes how pervasive the basic patterns are and the need to be careful about rapidly generalizing from one relationship episode, emphasizing that the psychotherapeutically significant general patterns appear most consistently in highly valued relationships.

3. Homework: Ask trainees to complete Form 24 (Relationship Episodes).

Session 4

Purpose: To review Form 24. The goal of this form is to help trainees learn how to use CCRT to perceive the patients' interpersonal patterns, including transference through relationship episode analysis.

1. Trainees are asked to report and discuss their ratings for each relationship episode. You can report the standard answers.

2. Trainees cannot be expected to get the "right answers" because they are not fully trained as researchers in rating relationship episodes. The aim is to help them break down interpersonal sequences in order to derive a pattern (CCRT).

3. Homework: Trainees are asked to read Appendix IV, "Sex, Love and Psychotherapy" and then to complete Form 25 (Questions about "Sex, Love and Psychotherapy").

Session 5

Purpose: To review trainees' reactions to "Sex, Love and Psychotherapy" and discuss Form 25. Doing Form 25 helps trainees recognize the signs and sources of transference and countertransference and increases their self-awareness of sexual feelings toward patients.

1. Start by asking about trainees' general reactions to the paper; and then discuss Form 25.

2. Most trainees do not want to believe that such things happen between therapist and patient. Intellectually, they recognize these things can happen, but they have trouble believing such intense responses could happen to them. They are surprised to learn how common sexual contact between psychotherapists and patients is. One trainee felt that if such reactions took place he would be responsible for them. This statement shows that CTX provides therapists with an opportunity to learn about themselves, since he acknowledged that he generally feels overly responsible for reactions of others to him. Other trainees cannot believe that discussion of such issues is possible, since sexual content is so difficult to discuss in any context.

Trainees want to know how to judge when to discuss transference. As with this patient, it should be discussed when it is directly relevant to the reasons the patient has sought help.

Trainees have less difficulty acknowledging feelings of excessive desire to nurture and rescue than sexual feelings and fantasies. We discuss how women therapists might be more vulnerable than men to the nurturing countertransference reaction.

Trainees often ask when the therapist should express his countertransference reaction to the patient. Ultimately, the answer depends on what is best for the patient and not the therapist. If the therapist needs to discuss the reaction, he or she should seek out supervision or consultation.

Session 6

Purpose: To watch the videotape vignettes showing transference and countertransference. We intend to have trainees watch the patient's attempts to elicit responses from the therapist and the therapist's responses to these efforts.

1. There are two vignettes: Dr. Beitman's session with J, and Dr. Beitman's report of his reactions to W. J is an obese woman with panic disorder, major depression, and a history of sexual abuse. She is currently living on welfare with her 12-year-old daughter in a trailer park. This was the twelfth session in a one-year period. W, is a married mother of two children, is dysthymic and has been socially isolated most of her life. Beitman's self-statement took place before the seventeenth session.

After group watches each vignette, direct the discussion to sign(s) of the patient's transference. What is the origin of the transference? Describe the interaction between the therapist and the patient. If you were the therapist, how would you handle the patient's transference in that situation? Does the therapist experience countertransference? From where does it come? Can you identify sign(s) of the therapist's countertransference? You may also encourage trainees to talk about their own experience with patients as they are reminded about them by the vignettes.

2. The session with J may induce frustration in some trainees. Discussion in our program has focused on the therapist's countertransference, which was demonstrated by his tone of voice and body language.

Trainees often have difficulty believing that the love discussion Beitman reports having with W can happen in psychotherapy. One group was silent for a long time after they watched the tape. They responded that it would be an extremely difficult situation for them to handle if it were to occur in their practice. The group discussed how and why this intense feeling between the therapist and the patient could occur in psychotherapy. One of our trainees shared the countertransference experience she had when a patient told her his fantasy of having sex with her. This trainee's experience seemed to shake the group's belief that erotic transference and countertransference would not happen to them. One trainee wanted to leave the office whenever patients said "tell me what I should do" to her. Two female trainees reported how strongly they want to take care of those patients who remind them of their brothers and sisters.

Watching Beitman's self-statement helps trainees gain awareness of the importance of monitoring their own thoughts and feelings toward patients. Generally they are touched by Dr. Beitman's willingness to examine his own feelings and appreciate his courage in showing his responses to the group.

3. Homework: Ask trainees to complete Form 26 (Analysis of Your Reactions to Other People).

Session 7

Purpose: To review Form 26, which provides another opportunity for trainees to observe their own interpersonal (not necessarily dysfunctional) patterns. We try to reinforce the observing self by asking them to examine their responses to one significant other and one patient.

1. The discussion of Form 26 challenges trainees to discuss their personal feelings. Some trainees may not be ready to share their experiences with the group. You can ask for a volunteer to start. As in group therapy, honesty should be nurtured; it helps trainees to understand each other, to support each other, and to share their feelings and experiences. Guide them to think about the sources of their reactions to each other and the similarities between their reactions to the significant other and to the patient.

2. Some trainees may obtain insights through the discussion. We believe this exercise improves trainees' personal growth. It may accomplish the goal of teaching trainees that they all form basic patterns in their intimate personal and professional relationships, helping them to see how these basic personal patterns impact on their reactions to their patients.

Several trainees in our groups saw parallels between their reactions to patients and their reactions to significant others. In describing reactions to relationships, two trainees saw the similarity between their reactions to their mothers, each of whom was underfunctioning and for whom the trainee felt the need to nurture and support. One of them thought it was "silly" that he had not seen the pattern of saving others as similar to that with his mother. It was suggested that "silly" protected him from having to recognize that he may be protecting his mother from his own anger at her.

Another trainee discovered that her reactions to her husband strongly resembled her relationship to one of her brothers "whom I loved a lot and fought with most of the time." She wondered why her relationship had reached this point with him, since it "did not start out this way." One trainee described how he "tried to give his son everything," perhaps because his father was a rigid disciplinarian and gave little. He began to wonder if he was giving too much to his son. The trainee had been overly giving to one of his patients.

3. Homework: Ask trainees to complete Form 27 (Transcript of Borderline Patients).

Session 8

Purpose: To review Form 27. This exercise uses borderline patients to trigger trainees' countertransference reactions and then helps them to identify, observe, and analyze these reactions. Again, we emphasize the use of the observing self.

1. After reading each transcript, trainees answer the questions. For the first question, trainees tend to analyze the patient's problems, rather than report the feelings that they experienced while reading the transcript. Ask them to project themselves into the therapist's role, then to focus on their emotional reactions to the patient and report them. The second question is intended to demonstrate similarities and differences in trainees' reactions to borderline patients. The differences can lead to the discussion of the sources of these unique reactions (the third question).

2. Case 1 of the suicidal patient often triggers anxiety and a sense of inadequacy in trainees. They are asked to consider that the sense of inadequacy might also be the experience of the patient (concordant countertransference).

The patient in case 2 triggers a sense of being devalued, anger (at being devalued), fear (that something bad would happen), and despair (of not helping the patient). Each of these feelings reflects a dominant emotion for each trainee.

Case 3 of the idealizing and then devaluing woman patient is usually more difficult for the men than for the women. Male trainees would have struggled to regain the idealized relationship. Woman trainees (when asked to think of the patient as a man) said that they remained objective with most patients, but if a man started to refer to them as "attractive," etc., they might feel quite uncomfortable. The group had trouble seeing that the therapist was not really "bored" but was reacting to the patient's discussing another man.

3. Homework: Ask trainees to complete Form 28 (Case Vignettes of Transference and Countertransference).

Session 9

Purpose: To review Form 28, the goal of which is to help trainees become familiar with different types of transference and countertransference. Also, when forced to categorize the types of transference and countertransference, trainees must consider carefully the origins of these responses.

1. Trainees are asked to report their answers. You can use Answers to Form 28 to facilitate the discussion, which should clarify different types of TX and CTX. You can focus on the cases to which trainees gave answers different from the standard answers.

2. Trainees seem to understand patient-originated and therapist-originated TX or CTX very well, but are often more confused about the interactive one.

3. Homework: Ask trainees to complete Form 29 (Transcripts of Transference).

Session 10

Purpose: To review Form 29, which teaches trainees how to manage patients' transference.

1. Form 29 reports an experienced therapist's responses to patients' transference. Ask trainees to project themselves as the therapist and think how they would respond to the patients.

2. Trainees come up with various responses to the patient and struggle with trying to find the "right answer." They need to be told that there are no "right answers." Emphasize learning more possibilities or new ways to respond to patients' transference.

Trainees' responses may reflect their interpersonal patterns. For example, one of our trainees used "why" repetitively instead of "how" to question the patient.

In our group, we examine the power of the here-and-now discussion of how "I feel about you." Dr. Beitman was able to show them a feeling of heightened awareness through an exercise in which trainees paired off and looked at each other, anticipating how the other might react. Their heart rates accelerated—we might call that anxiety but what was it?

One resident asked under what conditions, if any, would it be okay for a patient and therapist to be sexually involved. The group concluded that following the rule that under *no* conditions should they be involved was the safest.

Session 11

Purpose: To have trainees complete COSE (Post-module 6) and GI (Post-module 6), and review the training program. You need to complete GITC after this session.

Use the first 20 minutes for trainees to complete COSE (Post-module 6) and GI (Post-module 6). The rest of the session can be used to summarize the training and ask for feedback.

SUGGESTED ANSWERS TO FORM 23

Relationship Episodes from Ms. Smith

Session 3

RE #3: Brother and his wife

1. W: To get out of bad relationship (18, 23)
2. RO: Rejecting (4, 14)
   RO: Put down (6, 8)
3. RS: Feel bad about self (26, 17)
4. W: To be in good relationship (3, 2)
5. RS: Feel bad (22, 20)
6. RO: Dishonest (8, 15)
7. RO: Putting her down (8, 14)
8. RS: Anger (21, 6)

RE #4: Boyfriend

1. W: To stop bad relationship (18, 23)
2. RO: Rejecting (4, 14)
3. RS: Assertive about stopping, rejecting relationship (11, 14)
4. RO: Stopped talking to me (11, 14)
5. RO: Didn't contact me (12, 4)
6. RS: Anger (21, 6)
7. RS: I stop contact with him (18, 23)
8. RS: anger (21, 6)
9. RS: Reject other (6, 21)
10. W: Not be lonely again (11, 14)
11. RS: Lonely, crying (23?, 22?)
12. RS: Crying, sad (22, 23)
13. W: Not to feel isolated (11, 14?)
14. RS: Isolated (23, 20)
15. RS: Anger (21, 6)
16. RO: Other friend gave support (13, 3)
17. RO: Gave no support (14, 4)
18. RO: Gave no support (4, 14)

RE #5: Father

1. RO: Asshole (25?, 4?)
2. RO: Rejecting, nonsupportive (14, 4)
3 and 4. RO: Rejecting, nonsupportive, nonloving (14, 4)
5. RO: Noncaring (14, 4)
6. RS: Awareness of his nature (1?, 6?)
7. W: To get money (13, 8?)
8. RO: Nonsupportive (14? 4?)
9. W: To get money (13, 8)
10. RS: Shame about her asking for money (26, 25)
11. W: To end nonsupportive relationship (18, 23)
12. RO: Denies he is asshole (8? 2?)
13. RO: he is dishonest (8, 14?)

RE #6: Boss

1. RO: Nice people (13? 9?)
2. RS: Feel lucky (29? 28?)
3. RO: Together with Patient (3? 5?)
4. RS: It was nice (29, 28?)
5. RO: supports (13, 18?)
6. RO: Helps even at a sacrifice (13, 11)
7. RO: Concern (13, 3?)
8. W: Wish for concern and caring (13, 11)
9. RO: Concern about my feelings (13, 3?)
10. RO: Giving (13, 3?)
11. RO: Nice lady (11? 1?)
12. RS: Feel blessed (29? 28?)

Reprinted with permission from Luborsky, L. & Crits-Christoph, P. (1990). *Understanding Transference* (pp. 55–58). New York: Basic Books.

SUGGESTED ANSWERS TO FORM 24

From Mr. Howard, Age 20, Session 3

RE #1: Mother

RO: Disagrees with his view (7, 14)
W: To get sexual information (8?, 11?)
W: To get close to M. (11?, 8)
RO: (past) Explains (11, 13)
RO: Rejects (4, 12)
RS: Frustration (21, 20?)
RS: Shame (26, 25)

RE #2: Mother

RO: Disagrees with his view (7, 14)
RO: (past) Closeness (11?, 13?)
W: To be physically close (11, 8?)
RO: Rejection (4, 12)
RO: Choose someone else instead of P. (4, 12)

RE #3: Therapist

RS: Unresponsive, distant (8, 16?)
RS: Headache (31? —)
RS: Tense (27?, 9?)
RS: Lack of support or help (20, 17?)
Lack of response on his part (8, 16?)
RO: No rapport (12, 14?)
RO: No rapport (12, 14?)
RS: Lack of response on his part (8, 16?)

RE #4: Mother

W: To be close, have affection (11, 33)
RS: (past) Closeness, affection (30, 5)
RO: Blames (4, 14)
RS: Felt alone (23, 20?)

RE #5: Girlfriend

RS: Resentment (21, 20?)
W: To not suffer loss of relationships (11?, 33?)
RO: Cut off relationships (4, 14?)
RS: Fear of wish for attachment (?)
RO: Rejects (4?, 15)
RS: Blames self (25, 17?)

From Mr. Howard, age 20, Session 8

RE #1: Therapist

W: To be close (11, 17?)
RO: Forces me to give up girlfriend (24, 17?)
RS: Resentment (21, —)

Dream A: Trainers

W: To be close to trainer (therapist?) (11?, 27?)
RO: Stronger (24, —)
RO: Rejects (4, 17?)
RS: Not good enough (17, 20)

RE #2: Boyfriend

W: To trust, to share (6, 8) RO: Could screw me (8, 15)
W: To be close (11, 4?)

Dream B: Store

W: To be fed (13, 11?) RS: Sick (31?, ?)
RO: Too much ice cream (offered?) (? ?)

Dream C: Store owner

W: To buy something (13?, —) RO: Pursued by man (15, 4), stronger (24, —)
W: To expose self (33?, —)
RO: Shamed by ladies (4, 17)

RE #3: Therapist

W: To have trusting relationship (6, 3) RS: Distrust (6? 19?)
RO: Untrustworthy (8, 17?) RS: Self-blame (25, 26)

RE #4: Father

W: To get money (13?, 8?) RS: Distrust (20?, —)
RO: Does not give me (14, 4?)

Reprinted with permission from Luborsky, L. & Crits-Christoph. P. (1990). *Understanding Transference* (pp. 55–58). New York: Basic Books.

SUGGESTED ANSWERS TO FORM 28

1. Patient-originated transference.
2. Patient-originated transference; patient-originated countertransference (complementary countertransference)
3. Therapist-originated transference; therapist-originated countertransference
4. Therapist-originated countertransference
5. Therapist-originated countertransference
6. Patient-originated transference; patient-originated countertransference (complementary countertransference)
7. Patient-originated transference; patient-originated countertransference (complementary countertransference)
8. Patient-originated transference
9. Interactive transference; interactive countertransference
10. Patient-originated transference
11. Patient-originated countertransference (concordant countertransference)
12. Therapist-originated countertransference
13. Patient-originated transference; therapist-originated countertransference
14. Therapist-originated transference; therapist-originated countertransference

Posttraining

SESSIONS

During the posttraining period, each trainee produces an audiotape from the third session of two psychotherapy relationships to serve as a comparison for pretraining relationships. Data gathered from the posttraining is compared to pretraining, both to evaluate the training program and to measure each trainee's personal progress. Trainees can be asked, for example, to rate their own verbal response modes in the posttraining and to judge the difference between their range of responses, before and after.

Session 1

Purpose: To review forms to be completed by trainees and their patients after their third psychotherapy sessions.

1. You can go through the description of the first session in the text. While the forms to be completed are same as ones they used in pretraining, you still need to go through the details of how and when to use them, especially Form 6 (Rating the Therapist's Intentions) and Form 7 (Patient Reaction System). Suggest that trainees try to find patients whose diagnosis and other demographics match their pretraining patients (ideally, to match Form 2 profile of the patient in pretraining).

Session 2

Purpose: To gain feedback from trainees about their third psychotherapy session, especially their experiences of doing psychotherapy in pretraining and posttraining.

Afterword

Any book, course, or set of videotapes about psychotherapy has limitations, since the field is so broad and so deep. Our limitations are several:

1. The method of teaching through limited reading, much homework, and seminar discussion has many advantages. However, our method does not include more time-consuming but also valuable approaches, such as case conferences and in-depth reading of classical and practical papers and texts.
2. Our approach remains conceptual—practically conceptual but conceptual nevertheless. We do not attempt in-depth training in generic skills like empathic reflections and relaxation training or school-specific skills, including interpretation, cognitive restructuring, and role rehearsal. We do not teach trainees how to do these techniques, nor do we teach them when to use them.
3. We have not attempted to articulate a theory of normal human development, a theory of normal personality, a theory of psychopathology, or a comprehensive theory of treatment related to the previous theories. Ideally, but perhaps not necessarily, psychotherapy change models should be related to theories of normal and abnormal development. We await proof of this need, as well as the articulation of the relevant theories.
4. Several content areas that could be useful to all trainees are not covered. These include: assertiveness training, termination, combining pharmacotherapy and psychotherapy, culture and gender issues, as well as integrated approaches to a variety of *DSM-IV* diagnostic categories like major depression, panic disorder, and substance abuse.

In our opinion this training program fits well as an introduction to school-specific approaches. Ideally, these ideas are presented first and then trainees are taught cognitive therapy, interpersonal therapy, psychodynamic therapy, solution-focused therapies, and/or family therapy. Teachers of these and other approaches tend to believe that specific schools should be targeted for specific problems. While significant research evidence suggests that specific approaches treat specific problems, a broader view suggests that cognitive therapy (Lipsey & Wilson, 1993), for example, more resembles Prozac and its relatives Paxil and Zoloft (Schatzberg & Nemeroff, 1995) in that each is effective for a variety of diagnoses. Furthermore, practicing clinicians appear to combine what appears to them to be useful from different approaches to fit the perceived needs of their patients (Goldfried & Wolfe, 1996), including combining pharmacotherapy and psychotherapy (Beitman & Klerman, 1991). Therefore, we believe that a sophisticated psychotherapy integration, based upon the foundation presented here, lies in the future of psychotherapy education and practice.

Finally, we bring you back to the beginning. We believe that psychotherapy training should be fun! You learn about yourself while helping others; you study the human condition while serving humanity; you are involved in helping others find their ways through this confusing life and resolving some of your own misgivings and fears about living. To bring humor to the consulting room helps all participants. May fun and joy be part of your teaching and learning.

References

Alvarez, A. (1995). *Perceptions of fraudulence, counseling self-efficacy, and satisfaction with work.* Unpublished doctoral dissertation, State University at New York-Albany.

Bandura, A. (1986). (Ed.). *Social foundations of thought and action: A social cognitive theory.* Englewood Cliffs, NJ: Prentice Hall.

Beck, A., Rush, A., Shaw, B., & Emery, G. (1979). *Cognitive therapy of depression.* New York: Guilford.

Beitman, B. D., & Klerman, G. L. (Eds.). (1991). *Integrating pharmacotherapy and psychotherapy.* Washington, DC: American Psychiatric Press, Inc.

Binder, J. L., & Strupp, H. H. (1993). Recommendations for improving psychotherapy training based on experiences with manual-guided training and research: An introduction. *Psychotherapy, 30,* 571–572.

Bordin, E. S. (1979). The generalizability of the psychoanalytic concept of the working alliance. *Psychotherapy: Theory, Research and Practice, 16,* 252–260.

Breunlin, D. C., Schwartz, R. C., & Krause, M. S. (1989). The prediction of learning in family therapy training programs. *Journal of Marriage and Family Therapy, 15,* 387–395.

Daniels, J. A. (1997). *The influence of performance feedback and causal attributions upon ratings of counseling self-efficacy.* Unpublished doctoral dissertation, University of Nebraska-Lincoln.

DeGraaf, R. V. (1996). *Counselor self-efficacy development: An examination over time of the influence of trainee exposure to clients' negative affectivity and the supervisory alliance.* Unpublished doctoral dissertation, Loyola University, Chicago.

Dobson, K. S., & Shaw, B. F. (1993). The training of cognitive therapists: What have we learned from treatment manuals? *Psychotherapy, 30,* 573–577.

Garfield, S. L., & Bergin, A. E. (1971). Personal therapy, outcome and some therapist variables. *Psychotherapy: Theory, Research, and Practice, 8,* 252–253.

Garfield, S. L., & Kurtz, R. (1976). Personal therapy for the psychotherapist: Some findings and issues. *Psychotherapy: Theory, Research and Practice, 3,* 188–192.

Goldfried, M. R., & Wolfe, B. E. (1996). Psychotherapy practice and research: Repairing a strained alliance. *American Psychologist, 51,* 1007–1017.

Heppner, M. J., & O'Brien, K. M. (1997). Multicultural, counselor training students' perceptions of helpful and hindering events. *Counselor Supervision and Training, 34,* 4–18.

Heppner, P. P. & Mintz, L. B. (1997). *An intensive study of the change process in counseling.* Unpublished manuscript.

Heppner, P. P., Rosenberg, J. L., & Hedgespeth, J. (1992). Three methods in measuring the therapeutic process: Clients' and counselors' constructions of the therapeutic process versus actual therapeutic events. *Journal of Counseling Psychology, 39,* 20–31.

Larson, L. M. (1998a). The social cognitive model of counselor training. *The Counseling Psychologist, 26,* 219–273.

Larson, L. M. (1998b). Making it to the show: Four criteria to consider. *The Counseling Psychologist, 26,* 324–341.

Larson, L. M., Cardwell, T., & Majors, M. (1996, August). *Counseling self-efficacy, job satisfaction, and work environment: Predictors of burnout.* Paper presented at the American Psychological Association Convention in Toronto, Canada.

Larson, L. M., & Daniels, J. A. (1998). Review of the counseling self-efficacy literature. *The Counseling Psychologist, 26,* 179–218.

Larson, L. M., Suzuki, L., Gillespie, K., Potenza, M. T., Toulouse, A. L., & Bechtel, M. A. (1992). The development and validation of the counseling self-estimate inventory. *Journal of Counseling Psychology, 39,* 105–120.

Lipsey, M. W., & Wilson, D. B. (1993). The efficacy of psychological, educational, and behavioral treatment: Confirmation from a meta-analysis. *American Psychologist, 48,* 1181–1209.

Luborsky, L. (1993). Recommendations for training therapists based on manuals for psychotherapy research. *Psychotherapy, 30,* 578–580.

Luborsky, L., & Crits-Christoph, P. C. (1990). *Understanding transference.* New York: Basic Books.

Luborsky, L., McLellan, T., Woody, G. E., O'Brien, C., & Auerbach, A. (1985). Therapist success and its determinants. *Archives of General Psychiatry, 42,* 602–611.

Robertson, M. H. (1995). *Psychotherapy education and training: an integrative perspective.* Madison, CT: International Universities Press.

Sakinofsky, I. (1979). Evaluating the competence of psychotherapists. *Canadian Journal of Psychiatry, 24,* 193–205.

Schatzberg, A. F., & Nemeroff, C. B. (Eds.). (1995). *The American Psychiatry Press textbook of psychopharmacology.* Washington, DC: American Psychiatric Press, Inc.

White, N. K. (1996). *The relationship between counselor-trainee extra-therapy characteristics and success in counselor training.* Unpublished master's thesis, California State University, Chico, CA.